An Education That Empowers

BERA Dialogues

Series Editor: Donald McIntyre

Other Books in the Series

Please contact us for the latest book information:
Multilingual Matters Ltd, Frankfurt Lodge, Clevedon Hall,
Victoria Road, Clevedon, Avon BS21 7SJ, England

BERA Dialogues 10
Series Editor: Donald McIntyre

An Education That Empowers

A Collection of Lectures in Memory of
Lawrence Stenhouse

Edited by
Jean Rudduck

MULTILINGUAL MATTERS LTD
Clevedon • Philadelphia • Adelaide

Library of Congress Cataloging in Publication Data

An Education That Empowers: A Collection of Lectures in Memory of Lawrence
Stenhouse/Edited by Jean Rudduck
(BERA Dialogues: 10)
1. Stenhouse, Lawrence. 2. Education–Great Britain–Philosophy.
I. Rudduck, Jean. II. Stenhouse, Lawrence. III. Series.
LB880.S662E38   1995
370′.1–dc20   94-47423

British Library Cataloguing in Publication Data

A CIP catalogue record for this book is available from the British Library.

ISBN 1-85359-289-7 (hbk)
ISBN 1-85359-288-9 (pbk)

Multilingual Matters Ltd

UK: Frankfurt Lodge, Clevedon Hall, Victoria Road, Clevedon, Avon BS21 7SJ.
USA: 1900 Frost Road, Suite 101, Bristol, PA 19007, USA.
Australia: P.O. Box 6025, 83 Gilles Street, Adelaide, SA 5000, Australia.

Typeset by Proteus Microapplications.
Printed and bound in Great Britain by the Cromwell Press.

Contents

Foreword

After Lawrence Stenhouse's death in 1982 a Memorial Appeal was set up by William Etherington, Dean of the School of Education at the University of East Anglia where Stenhouse was Professor of Education and Director of CARE (the Centre for Applied Research in Education). The first event that the Appeal supported — something that Lawrence Stenhouse had requested before he died — was a workshop that brought together teachers and doctors to look at the way in which illness and death might be handled in schools. Jane Abercrombie was a key speaker and a local group of drama teachers presented incidents for discussion.

The next Dean, Hugh Sockett, established a Memorial Trust Committee which decided to sponsor some lectures in Stenhouse's name. The first two were given informally to staff and students at CARE by Malcolm Skilbeck and Jean Rudduck. In 1988, Geoffrey Brown, the then Dean and Chair of the Memorial Committee discussed with the British Educational Research Association (BERA) the possibility that the lectures should be given at the annual BERA conferences which are usually held in early September — coincidentally, the time of year when Lawrence Stenhouse died.

The first BERA Memorial Lecture was given by John Elliott at the 1988 BERA conference which was held at the University of East Anglia. The following year the conference took place at the University of Newcastle and Stephen Kemmis gave the lecture. In 1990 Brian Simon was the speaker and BERA met that year at the Roehampton Institute, London. The next lecturer was Tony Edwards, who spoke at the conference held at what was then Trent Polytechnic. In 1992, the tenth anniversary of Lawrence Stenhouse's death, BERA met in Scotland, at the University of Stirling, and Donald McIntyre gave the lecture. (In this collection, the papers are not reproduced in the order in which they were given.)

I should like to thank the BERA Executive for their encouragement to produce this edited volume, the Memorial Trust Committee (now under John Elliott's chairmanship) for their agreement and support, and the five speakers for their generous collaboration.

Jean Rudduck
Spring, 1994

Acknowledgements

The five lectures reprinted here were originally produced as separate booklets (School of Education Publications, University of East Anglia) for the Lawrence Stenhouse Memorial Trust.

John Elliott's lecture has also been printed in his book, *Action Research for Educational Change*, published by the Open University Press, 1991.

Brian Simon's lecture has also been printed in *What Future for Education?*, published by Lawrence and Wishart Ltd.

About the Contributors

Tony Edwards is Dean of Education at the University of Newcastle where he has been Professor of Education since 1979. Recent publications include (with David Westgate) *Investigating Classroom Talk* (Falmer Press, second edition 1994) and (with Geoff Whitty and Sharon Gewitz) *Specialisation and Choice in Urban Education* (Routledge, 1993).

John Elliott is Professor of Education and Dean of the School of Education at the University of East Anglia. He is consultant for the Organisation for Economic Co-operation and Development (OECD) on international curriculum development and environmental education. Recent publications include *Action Research for Educational Change* (Open University Press, 1991) and (as editor) *Reconstructing Teacher Education* (Falmer Press, 1991).

Stephen Kemmis is Professor of Education and Head of the Graduate School of the Faculty of Education, Deakin University, Geelong, Australia. He is co-author (with Wilfred Carr) of *Becoming Critical: Education, Knowledge and Action Research* (Falmer, 1986) and (with Robin McTaggart) of *The Action Research Planner* (third edition, Deakin University Press, 1988). He is author of *Curriculum Theorising* (Deakin University Press, 1986).

Donald McIntyre is Reader in Education at the Department of Education, University of Oxford. Recent publications include (with Sally Brown) *Making Sense of Teaching* (Open University Press, 1993), (with Hazel Hagger and Katharine Burn) *The School Mentor Handbook* (Kogan Page, 1993) and *Managing School-Based Teacher Education* (Kogan Page, 1994), and as co-editor (with Hazel Hagger and Margaret Wilkin) *Mentoring: Perspectives on School-Based Teacher Education* (Kogan Page, 1993).

Brian Simon is Emeritus Professor of Education, University of Leicester. Recent publications (all published by Lawrence & Wishart) include *Education and the Social Order* (1991), *Bending the Rules, the Baker 'Reform' of Education* (1988), *What Future for Education?* (1992) and (with Clyde Chitty) *SOS, Save Our Schools* (1993). A collection of his writings and lectures, *The State and Educational Change: Essays in the History of Education and Pedagogy*, was published in 1994.

Introduction

JEAN RUDDUCK

Of whom shall we speak? For every day they die
Among us, those who were doing us some good.
(Auden, November 1939)[1]

Born in Scotland, Lawrence Stenhouse completed his secondary education at Manchester Grammar School but returned to Scotland — to St Andrew's University — as an undergraduate. He later studied at Glasgow University and by the time he completed his M.Ed. in 1956 he had defined the educational problem that he wanted to work on as 'the relationship of culture to the development of the power of the individual'; later, this agenda was more sharply expressed as 'the problem of emancipation through knowledge'.

His secondary education had been particularly influential in shaping this agenda. He recalled several teachers 'who had opened ideas . . . in a way that emancipated me by enhancing my sense of my own powers'. When he eventually started to teach, he discovered 'that though the school system valued achievement narrowly defined, it did not for the most part value the emancipation of pupils through knowledge'. He continued to see education as constrained by traditional assumptions about access to knowledge. He had himself attended 'a privileged school, where knowledge and the power associated with it were represented to me as my right', but he was teaching in schools 'where the message was that many are called but few are chosen'.

He left teaching to become a lecturer in secondary education at the Institute of Education at Newcastle-upon-Tyne and then principal lecturer at Jordanhill College of Education, Glasgow. In 1966 he visited the United States to attend a conference and there he met Joslyn Owen, a leading figure at the new Schools Council for Curriculum and Examinations in London. As a result of this meeting he was invited to apply for the directorship of The Humanities Project, which was to be jointly funded by the Schools Council and the Nuffield Foundation. He was thus given the chance to transform an educationally important set of ideas into strategies that teachers could use and learn from in their classrooms.

1

The Humanities Project was one of the most controversial and most influential projects of the curriculum development movement in the UK. It brought together a number of Lawrence Stenhouse's interests: the right of the student to knowledge; the connectedness of school knowledge with the student's understanding of the world outside school; the disciplined use of evidence as a basis for judgement; the importance of discussion as a way of exploring ideas in collaborative company.

Towards the end of the project, he and several of his colleagues moved to the University of East Anglia to set up the Centre for Applied Research in Education, CARE, which established a national and international reputation for research that addressed the problems of practice and for its commitment to the idea of the teacher as researcher. There, in 1975, he produced his major book, *An Introduction to Curriculum Research and Development*.[2] His research activities focused mainly on curriculum but later he moved on to develop a substantial body of work on the theory and practice of case study and, in particular, how school and classroom studies can be used to support teachers in developing their understanding of what is possible in the classroom (see Burgess & Rudduck)[3].

Just before he died in 1982 he put together a collection of his papers called *Authority, Education and Emancipation*[4] — a title that powerfully summarises the themes that united his work across the years.

The Memorial Lecture

Lawrence Stenhouse thought highly of the European tradition of the *Festskrift*. The logic of the *Festskrift* is that a collection of essays is produced that celebrates a person's achievements while she or he is still around to enjoy the tribute. Sadly, Lawrence's early death in 1982 left us with only the possibility of paying our respects through a series of memorial lectures. In 1988, the BERA annual conference became the occasion of these lectures and the first five are collected in this volume.

The once-robust tradition of funeral oratory has weakened over the years and, generally speaking, we are not very good now at the constructive use of the memorial occasion. The sermons of the seventeenth century[5] were often strikingly aggressive in their challenge to the power of Death, but the funeral address today, at what is essentially a private family event, tends to be more compliant and consoling. For public figures the newspaper obituary is the expected honour; generally genteel and subdued, it offers immediate homage without, usually, referring to the cause or manner of death. For our warriors it is different: for them we have a tradition of communal remembrance but, moving as the annual service at the Cenotaph is, and the soft fall of the poppies at the Royal Albert Hall, we do not seize the moment and transmute the reverence into energy — as they did, for instance, in ancient Athens. According to Thucydides,[6] the high point of the ceremony was the funeral oration, and the occasion was used (if we can generalise from the performance of Pericles) for an impassioned affirmation of Athenian commitment to the values of freedom and democracy.

We do not have such powerful traditions to call on in our academic memorial lectures — although, as you will see, those collected here are not without their passion — but, as in Athens, the speakers were all chosen for their 'intellectual gifts and general reputation'.

The memorial lectures will continue as part of the BERA annual conference and as time passes they will become increasingly depersonalised for neither speakers nor audience will be as familiar with Lawrence Stenhouse's work as many of us are today. But, for the moment, and as a context for the lectures themselves, I want to recall some aspects of his thinking about teachers and about students that seem relevant to the situation that we find ourselves in the 1990s.

On Teachers

Lawrence Stenhouse's work gives the lie to claims of the new right that poor standards in schools today are traceable to the slack progressivism of curriculum development in the 1960s and 70s. He was one of the leading figures in the curriculum development movement of that period and his work is characterised by a profound respect for thinking that is disciplined by evidence, by respect for the centrality of knowledge, by a commitment to 'form' — and therefore 'formality' — in classroom pedagogy, and by the projection of high aspirations for students. Above all, he maintained trust in the teacher as a professional — something which the present (Conservative) government has signally failed to do (Donald McIntyre's lecture offers a strong reaffirmation of trust in the teacher). Alongside the quality of the structures for thinking about practice that Stenhouse offered teachers, the confusion and incompetence that has marked the present government's planning and implementation of curriculum reform is astonishing — almost surreal. The national curriculum and the associated programme of testing have created considerable ambiguity about the status of teachers; the problem seems to be to find the right balance between freedom and framework: enough support to ensure continuities of learning for students across the country and enough guidance to support teachers who are new to the profession — but also enough intellectual challenge to enable both new and experienced teachers to refine professional judgement.

Lawrence Stenhouse would have agreed, I think, with a sentence in the Crowther Report (1959),[7] 'Everything in education depends ultimately on the teacher'. It is not insignificant that teachers whom he had worked with in East Anglia contributed to a plaque in his memory on which they inscribed his own words: 'It is the teachers who in the end will change the world of the school by understanding it.'[8] As Malcolm Skilbeck said: 'His theory of education is

essentially a theory of teacher professionalism, autonomy and development.'
Skilbeck went on:

> It is the teacher, purposive and free, informed by knowledge and
> understanding, with clearly articulated values, and a repertoire of practical
> skills, that he saw as the central agent in the educational enterprise and the
> ultimate focus of his views on research.[9]

As Skilbeck suggests, the common ground in Stenhouse's 'views on research'
— whether he was cavalierly attacking the positivist paradigm, or thinking about
case study, or arguing for research-based teaching, or exploring the idea of 'the
teacher as researcher' — tended to be the way that research could enhance teachers'
professional understanding. The most enduring idea — and, as Kemmis (Chapter
5) shows, the most unfinished — is the idea of the teacher as researcher. It seemed,
originally, reasonably straightforward. Teachers are researchers in the sense that
they are always trying to get better at teaching by consciously identifying some
significanct aspect of practice that they need to understand better and to work
on. They learn by careful enquiry into their own practice and, where possible,
by bringing to bear on practice ideas from research and from some kinds of
educational theory.

Over time, the idea of teacher research has become snarled up, along with
'reflective practice' and 'action research', in over-intricate webs of meaning;
perhaps too many of us have been trying to define it rather than help teachers
do it. But there were some weaknesses in Stenhouse's perspective, as Kemmis
points out in his lecture. It was not clear, for instance, whether teachers were
to contribute to public knowledge by writing about their work or whether it was
enough that they deepen their own understanding and enhance their own practice.
Nor was it clear whether the role of the practitioner in relation to theory-building
was merely to test, in the laboratory of the classroom, the ideas of the 'professional'
researchers. Kemmis offers a timely review of these issues — and a resolution
— in his lecture. It is perhaps enough to say, here, that in emphasising the idea
of the teacher as researcher Stenhouse was trying to suggest that the quality of
teachers' work should not be static but rather be continually advanced — by the
teacher her or himself. 'What is needed is progress in the art of teaching as a
public tradition and a personal achievement',[10] he said, and what he meant, I
am sure, was something different from moving on to the next level of competence.

Stenhouse was an outspoken critic of the cult of teacher deprofessionalisation
which, in the early 1970s, used the 'teacher proof curriculum package' and/or
the objectives model as its vehicle. Of the objectives model he said:

> I believe [it] actually rests on an acceptance of the teacher as a kind of
> intellectual navvy. An objectives based curriculum is like a site-plan, simplified

so that people know exactly where to dig their trenches without having to know why.[11]

He regarded the objectives model as appropriate only for a limited range of learning activities — such as the mastery of skills — and was dismayed to see it being hi-jacked into activities designed to support the extension of students' knowledge and understanding (John Elliott takes up this theme in his lecture, Chapter 4). The objectives model was, for him, a symbol of distrust of the teacher and he was ready to confront and challenge any approach to curriculum design and implementation that sidelined teachers: 'It seems odd', he wrote, 'to attempt to minimise the use of the most expensive resource in the school.'[12] He acknowledged that not all schools and not all teachers are as successful as they might be in giving direction to and sustaining children's learning, but the only way forward, for him, was to reinvest in the teacher, and to construct the curriculum in ways that would enhance teachers' understanding and capability.

Students benefit from curriculum development through the updating of knowledge and through the reframing of content in ways that enable them to make better sense of what they learn. But they also benefit because involvement in curriculum change, properly handled, enables teachers to improve. Improvement comes — or should come — because curriculum development is about *ideas*: it offers a set of propositions about practice that the teacher can work on in his or her own setting. Thus the teacher learns from the insights about teaching and learning that involvement in educationally justifiable innovation yields. What is so disconcerting about much centralised reform is that it is so short on ideas that would take teachers — and students — forward.

On Students

Lawrence Stenhouse seldom wrote directly and at length about students; he invariably focused on teachers. But when passages about students and their learning are brought together from various sources they constitute an important and radical statement.

Empowerment is a word that has recently lost some of its rallying power — perhaps because we have come to think of it, pessimistically, as an impossible aim in the present climate. We see, now, the resurgence of various forms of differentiation, fuelled by the government's commitment to the principle of competition as a basis for achievement. As Meece[13] has said, 'Competition pits student against student, and the scarcity of meaningful rewards for those who cannot achieve competitively undermines teacher–student relations and discourages "marginal" students'. Stenhouse's word — and a stronger one — was 'emancipation'. As he said,[14] it is all too easy for policy makers to think of students only as 'means and standard deviations'; his interest was both more personal and more ambitious:

My theme is an old-fashioned one; emancipation. In its roots, the *Oxford English Dictionary* tells us, it is, in Roman law, the action of or process of setting children free from the *patrias potestas*, the parental jurisdiction. But this is a mere nominal freeing unless it be supported by another definition the dictionary offers: delivering from intellectual, moral, or spiritual fetters. The essence of emancipation, as I conceive it, is the intellectual, moral and spiritual autonomy which we recognise when we eschew paternalism and the rule of authority and hold ourselves obliged to appeal to judgment. Emancipation rests not merely on the assertion of a right of the person to exercise intellectual, moral and spiritual judgment, but upon the passionate belief that the virtue of humanity is diminished in man when judgment is overruled by authority.[15]

He was concerned, throughout his working life, to trace the practical implications of emancipation for the relationship of students to knowledge, of students to teachers and of students to schools.

Students and knowledge

The exploration of the relationship between knowledge, authority and emancipation was the central concern of the Humanities Project and also the central concern of Stenhouse's later study of sixth formers and libraries. What Stenhouse sought to challenge, in both contexts, were well-intentioned but misguided simplifications of knowledge, and the related problem of limiting 'literacy' by setting goals that underestimate students' potential for thinking.

His approach to the idea of 'entitlement' was markedly more robust and challenging than the easily contradicted rhetorics of today: he called for 'an aspiration towards a knowledge-based education at every stage of schooling and for everyone'.[16] Literacy, in his view, is a fundamental right of every child; but it is not just about mastering the basics of reading, writing and number; such mastery is crucially important but there is a broader, intellectual literacy which functions as a gate which 'lets people into the means of thinking for themselves and becoming critical of our society'[17] (a theme taken up in the lectures given by Brian Simon, John Elliott and Tony Edwards). He accepted that the teaching profession had a responsibility, however difficult, 'to struggle with the consequences of that ambition'. One consequence, of course, is that knowledge gives power to the dispossessed, an outcome that not all governments are happy to endorse. By and large, he concluded, most schools have been allowing students only 'such an acquaintance with knowledge as might be expected to inculcate a respect for those who are knowledgeable. Their lot has been to accept that truths are defined by the authority of others'.[18] Or, as he put it elsewhere, the problem is that from an early age 'we learn to be subservient to other people's ideas, be in awe of the learned, and to mistake the printed word for the truth. The process of learning to value oneself in relation to knowledge, to achieve confidence in one's own construction of reality, to begin, however tentatively, to own knowledge ... is, however, crucially important'.[19] Quite often we find that students are so protected from the nature of knowledge that they can be shocked by the disorder that is suddenly apparent in a world that teachers have made orderly for them.

Stenhouse's commitment to intellectual honesty in teaching and learning led him to argue that students should be helped, from an early age, to accept that knowledge is provisional. It follows that it is important to make sure that they experience sound procedures for examining evidence and modifying views in the light of evidence. He saw many teachers offering their students a protective safety-net of facts and certainties and encouraging in them a distrust of doubt. (Tony Edwards, Chapter 3, discusses the issue of certainty in relation to school knowledge and also in relation to research knowledge.)

Stenhouse's position is nicely echoed in some passages from Wynne Harlen's presidential address to BERA members in 1993.[20] She suggests that 'those at the forefront in natural science and the social sciences share a common view of new knowledge as being the best current hypothesis which is always open to change'. She goes on: 'Thus science is no longer to be characterised as being objective, capable of yielding ultimate truths, "proving" things ... .' Instead, science is to be seen as a *human* activity which:

- seeks to advance understanding of the world around
- depends on human judgement
- is a social enterprise
- builds upon previous knowledge and understanding
- uses a wide range of methods of enquiry
- produces understanding which is tentative and always open to challenge by further evidence
- is constrained by values
- is subject to social determination of the acceptability of its conclusions.

Of course, there will be some scientists — and some teachers — who do not think this way — but 'the future is not on their side', she warns.

What schooling was about, for Lawrence Stenhouse, was access to knowledge for all students 'on terms that confer the power to use it'.

Students and teachers

Stenhouse wanted teachers to be ambitious for their students. 'The overall aim of education is to enable students to create unpredictable achievements which can lay claim to excellence', he said,[21] and his curriculum work was designed to help teachers see 'how far ordinary students can in fact be taken'.[22] It is particularly interesting today, in the context of the debates about school effectiveness, performance indicators and attainment targets, to review his vision of a learning partnership that has at its heart high aspirations for students.

The crucial element is respect. Stenhouse was confident that students would do better in school if they were treated with respect as learners. Respect can be signalled in different ways. It is communicated when teachers listen to students and are prepared to take their ideas seriously. It is demonstrated in the care teachers take to ensure that curriculum content links in important ways with students' own lives and developing perspectives. And it is reflected in the extent to which teachers make accessible to students the logic behind the structures and procedures that shape, but often remain implicit in, classroom practice. In some respects, his thinking echoes Dewey who said: 'There is no defect in traditional education greater than its failure to secure the active co-operation of the pupil in the construction of the purposes involved in his [sic] studying'.[23]

The concern not to underestimate students was a major theme in Stenhouse's work. For instance, he was wary of simplifying things; simplification can communicate low expectations of students and it can trivialise content. Instead, Stenhouse wanted teachers to help students to struggle with difficulty, to enjoy the challenge of things that are 'hard', and to feel that if they struggle with meaning, then they are gaining: failure is about avoiding struggle. He would have shared the view that education should not be like putting a coin in a vending machine and getting a chocolate bar. And he would surely have been in sympathy with Sarason[24] who asked why we are not deeply upset 'that so many students come to view the life of the mind, the world of ideas ... as derogated arenas of experience'. Changes in the structures of schooling do not seem to have kept pace with the earlier maturity of young people; and the new curriculum frameworks that we have in this country have, perhaps, not given sufficient thought to ways of knowing that stretch children's minds, and to ways of connecting school knowledge with the students' worlds outside school. What Sarason says of reform in the US is true of reform here:

> The educational reform movement has not come to grips with (these) overarching aims. One can alter curricula, change power relationships, raise standards ... but if these efforts are not powered by altered conceptions of what makes (students) tick and keeps them intellectually alive, willingly pursuing knowledge and growth, their results will be inconsequential.[25]

Interestingly, Stenhouse was writing in the 1960s about standards[26] and how they could be used to help students develop a stronger sense of control over their own learning — but the values that informed his discussion were somewhat different from the values that structure the debate about standards today. By 'standards' he meant 'the criteria adopted in the criticism of classrooms, and not levels of attainment in classwork'.[27] He went on: 'Whenever classroom behaviour or classroom work is judged, standards are implied, and within the classroom there are at least two different standards operative, that of the class and that of the teacher'.[28] He urged teachers to discuss criteria for judgement with students so that the students themselves might begin to understand how judgements of excellence are constructed and how they might more confidently use the criteria for judgement in relation to their own work.[29]

All this sounds very formal and indeed that was the intention. Stenhouse favoured formality because, given unequal power relations in the classroom, informality usually privileges the teacher while formality tends to be more respectful of the status of the student. His was not an arid formality, however; he was all for enjoyment and humour in the classroom but he saw the relationship between teacher and student as essentially 'contractual': 'It *can* be personal, but only if the personal tone of the relationship is not used to smooth the way to slackness of contract'.[30] The 'contract' should oblige teachers to offer students more information about, and opportunities to discuss, not only criteria for judgement but also the logics of different ways of working in the classroom, and where particular courses of study are heading. As Stenhouse pointed out, the unexamined authority regime of schools leads teachers to neglect to offer explanations and justifications — particularly when routines change:

> No experiment can be mounted without its purposes, duration and criteria being presented to pupils and without their being invited to monitor its effects on them, both in process and in outcome.[31]

A contractual relationship should protect students from the personal bias of the teacher for it means that the teacher must work 'to the full advantage of the child he or she dislikes as of the child he or she likes'[32]; equally, a student should work well for a teacher he or she does not like — provided that the teacher is fair and professionally skilful. Stenhouse would often talk about the possibility of helping students to see that instead of playing up the novice teacher or the teacher whose classroom control is easily shaken, they might think how they could, together, make the best of what the teacher has to offer — otherwise they are wasting their time and the teacher's, and disadvantaging themselves in terms of their right to learn.

Students and schools

Stenhouse emphasised not only the social responsibilities of the student to the school and its members, and the student's responsibility to learn, but also the *demands* that the student might properly make of the school; he believed that the school should behave fairly and responsibly to all its students. In 1975 he produced a catechism of these 'demands'.[33] Students:

- have a right to demand that the school shall treat them impartially and with respect as persons.
- have a right to demand that the school's aims and purposes shall be communicated to them openly, and discussed with them as the need arises.
- have a right to demand that the procedures and organisational arrangements of the school should be capable of rational justification and that the grounds of them should be available to them.
- have a right to expect that the school will offer them impartial counsel on academic matters, and if they desire it, with respect to personal problems.
- who live in home or environmental circumstances which make it difficult for them to meet the demands which the school from time to time places on them have a right to expect special consideration and compassion from the school.
- have a right to expect that the school will make unabated efforts to provide them with the basic skills necessary for living an autonomous life in our society.
- have a right to expect that the school will provide them with a general education which will equip them to enter upon a job and which will provide an adequate basis for further specialised education and training. Where unemployment is high, the school cannot meet the first of these demands, and morale suffers without the school having it in its power to remedy the situation.
- have a right to expect that the school will do its best to make available to them the major public traditions in knowledge, arts, crafts and sports, which form the basis of a rich life in an advanced society.
- have a right to expect that the school will enable them to achieve some understanding of our society as it stands and that it will equip them to criticise social policy and contribute to the improvement of society.

In many schools and classrooms it would be difficult for teachers to take on board the full implications of Stenhouse's aspirations for their work with students. Sadly, the recent reforms lack the intellectual integrity that would enable them to support teachers in taking seriously the broad idea of student 'entitlement'.

The Five Lectures

The first of the lectures collected here was given in 1988 — the year of the Education Reform Act. The implications of the Act and of subsequent legislation that carries through the principle of 'choice and diversity' into other areas of the education system continue to dominate debate; it is not surprising therefore to find the four speakers from our own education system reflecting on some aspects of Stenhouse's work on teachers and the school curriculum in the light of the recent policy changes. Brian Simon focuses on what is happening in schools, Donald McIntyre on what is happening in teacher education, and Tony Edwards on both teaching and teacher education. John Elliott concentrates on the recapture of education by the logic of technical rationality, and the need to reconstruct teaching as a social act. Stephen Kemmis, although not responding directly to the provocations and possibilities of the Education Reform Act, argues, in a timely way, the importance of rethinking the idea of the teacher as researcher and of the relationship of higher education staff and teachers to each other and to educational research.

Brian Simon's concern (Chapter 1) is with what is happening to schools, pupils and the curriculum as a result of the 1988 Act. An early advocate of the idea of a common curriculum, Simon urges us to 'seize on what is positive, or what can be made positive, in recent legislation'. He recalls Sir Peter Newsam's observation that for all its weaknesses the national curriculum, in principle, seeks for all young people 'a common set of educational experiences pitched at a high level'. The setting up of structures in support of such an aspiration would undoubtedly be judged to be 'the most important achievement of the 1980s'. However, what worries Simon is the translation of principle into practice. There is already evidence of aspects of policy that contradict the central idea of a common curriculum and that call into question the belief that the government actually has 'the educational interests of the mass of children' at heart.

In relation to the idea of 'entitlement', says Simon, 'Lawrence Stenhouse had something very significant to say', and he takes up the idea (one that Tony Edwards also recalls at the close of his paper) of an education that will help all young people learn to think for themselves and give them the confidence to believe that they matter and that what they know and what they think matters. However, it is increasingly apparent that the fears that Brian Simon expressed in his lecture were well founded: in the context of sharp competition for reputation and resources, schools are experiencing pressure to differentiate structures for learning and through them to deny the full range of opportunity to some pupils. Once again, it seems, as Lawrence Stenhouse noted more than a decade ago, the education that empowers is likely to be 'an education reserved for privilege'.

Donald McIntyre (Chapter 2) treads a different path; he focuses on teacher education and recent government proposals to give greater responsibility for the education and training of student teachers to practising teachers, and to base more of the work in schools. As he says, this is an appropriate subject for the Memorial Lecture 'not because it was one of Lawrence Stenhouse's major areas of interest . . . but because teachers' work certainly was'.

McIntyre's paper offers the kind of thoughtful, balanced and informed understanding that the govenment *should* have drawn on in exploring the possibilities and problems of a move to a more teacher-centred and school-based structure for initial teacher education. While welcoming the opportunity for teachers to be more equal partners in the process, he is properly critical of the simplistic views of initial teacher education that have shaped policy. He quotes Lawlor, for instance, who, he says, seems to believe 'that successful school teaching depends, like a successful day at the races, on only a few good tips'. Moreover, the idea that expertise in teaching needs only practice to feed on is 'quite inadequate'; it does not take account of the complex 'cognitive and affective developments' involved in learning to teach and in becoming a better teacher.

Central to McIntyre's exploration of his theme is the idea — developed by Lawrence Stenhouse — that teachers develop professional understanding and expertise by careful reflection on their own practice. Without frameworks to guide reflection, practice becomes only 'directionless experience' — of the kind that the government, in its presentation of the case for curriculum reform, was properly impatient of. He shares Stenhouse's views that the improvement of practice is an intellectually demanding undertaking, and that tutors in higher education have a distinctive contribution to make to the gradual refinement of professional insight and judgement.

Tony Edwards (Chapter 3) takes one motif from Lawrence Stenhouse's work — the idea of knowledge as uncertain and provisional, and another from Donald Schon's work — his presentation of classrooms as 'messy and indeterminate' settings for the practice of teaching and learning. Edwards brings these two perspectives together in support of a view of teaching and teacher education in which learning through disciplined reflection on practice is a basis for the improvement of practice.

Never before, he says, has education been 'so plagued by certainties' — and, at the level of policy, so untroubled by an awareness of the need for research and for informed understanding of the situations and structures that are the target of change. Like McIntyre, Edwards challenges the simplistic notion that what is involved in learning to teach is merely the 'unproblematic passing on, or passing down, of what the experienced teacher knows'. As one might predict for educational reform that is not based on research, complex learning processes tend to be reduced to a simple travesty of themselves. Schon and Stenhouse, in contrast, were properly realistic in basing their work on a recognition of the complexity of the task of teaching and the complexity of the institutional and personal contexts of learning to teach. What education deserves, concludes Edwards, are policy makers who are reluctant to undertake radical change without first committing themselves to the 'labour of understanding', and who are prepared to become practised 'in taking research seriously' and using it as a basis for planning.

'The logic of "technical rationality" pervades the Educational Reform Act' argues John Elliott (Chapter 4). It is evident in the current preoccupation with 'standards' and 'standardisation' and is particularly dominant in the construction of an agenda of achievement which emphasises conformity and predictability and fails to respect the importance of individual creativity. It supports the idea of an 'education for having' rather than an 'education for being'.

We can, Elliott argues, 'draw on the legacy of Stenhouse's ideas' in formulating an appropriate response. He recalls the debates of the late 1960s and early 1970s when technical rationality was embodied in the objectives model of curriculum development and was challenged by Lawrence Stenhouse. The process model was articulated then as an *educational* alternative for aspirations that went beyond skills-related, easily definable and easily measurable outcomes. Echoing Stenhouse, Elliott sets high aims for pupils and for teachers, calling for a pedagogy that emphasises such qualities as 'curiosity, patience, tenacity, persistence, open-mindedness, intellectual courage, honesty with oneself, humility'. The values that underpinned the old 'process model' are needed, Elliott suggests, to spearhead another phase of necessary critique and to help construct a context in which education can be viewed as a social practice rather than as a technical accomplishment.

The authors of the first four papers collected here identified some aspect of Lawrence Stenhouse's thinking about the curriculum or about teachers that was consonant with their own concerns and they brought it into the current educational arena on the grounds that the thinking was still relevant. Stephen Kemmis (Chapter 5), however, takes a different focus — educational research and, in particular, teacher research — and a different stance. While acknowledging the influence of Stenhouse's work, Kemmis looks back on him as a 'transitional figure' — someone who bravely confronted issues that were significant in the 1960s and 1970s (and that remain significant today) but who was inevitably bound into his time. Developments since his death have made it possible to look at these issues in a different way.

Stenhouse's achievement, he suggests, was to ensure that it is no longer possible to think about improving schools 'simply as a matter of changing the resources available to teachers, or even in terms of changing what teachers do'. He recognised, says Kemmis, that 'large-scale curriculum research and development did not necessarily bring improvements in local educational practice, and that it would always require teacher research ... to achieve lasting improvements in the quality of education'. But definitions of the roles and relationships, in research, of school teachers and higher education staff must be re-examined.

What we need, Kemmis argues, is a different perception of 'the concrete, material practices through which we educational researchers relate to educational practitioners'. What he offers is 'a reconstruction of metapractices' — that is, those social practices which structure, constrain and constitute the conditions for the practice of educational research. He emphasises the importance of debate and the right to participate in debate, for 'thought ... becomes knowledge, and knowledge is accommodated in theory ... by being tested, justified and sustained through a *social process* of debate'.

Kemmis's lecture serves as a timely reminder of the way in which our current practices are subverted by such frameworks as the 'research selectivity exercise', which puts pressure on us to place our ideas — urgently, discretely and in writing — in the public arena without our necessarily having any sense of participation in a communal debate. By accepting such pressures we are contributing to the deconstruction of education as a social practice.

As Kemmis said, Stenhouse's voice was an eloquent expression of the issues that structured debate when he was alive; we need other voices, now, to structure and sustain the debate. The writers in this book, between them, offer a range of ideas which, as Kemmis says, educational researchers and educational research associations, teachers — and, desirably, policy makers — should think about together in order to find educationally acceptable ways of enhancing the educational experience of young people and their teachers.

Notes and references

1. Auden, W.H. (1979) *Selected Poems* (edited by E. Medelson). London: Faber & Faber.
2. Stenhouse, L.A. (1975) *An Introduction to Curriculum Research and Development.* London: Heinemann.
3. Burgess, R.G. and Rudduck, J. (eds) (1993) *A Perspective on Educational Case Study.* CEDAR Papers 4, University of Warwick.
4. Stenhouse, L.A. (1983) *Authority, Education and Emancipation.* London: Heinemann Educational Books.
5. Carey, J. (1981) *John Donne: Life, Mind and Art.* London: Faber & Faber.
6. Thucydides (translated by Rex Warner) (1978 edition) *The Peloponnesian War.* Harmondsworth: Penguin Books.
7. Central Advisory Council for Education (The Crowther Report) (1959) *15 to 18*, Vol. 1. London: HMSO.
8. Stenhouse, L.A. (1975) *An Introduction to Curriculum Research and Development*, p. 208.
9. Skilbeck, M. (1983) Lawrence Stenhouse: Research methodology. *British Educational Research Journal* 9 (1), 12.
10. Stenhouse, L.A. (1979) Research as a basis for teaching (an inaugural lecture), reprinted in L.A. Stenhouse (1983) *Authority, Education and Emancipation*, op. cit., p. 189.
11. Stenhouse, L.A. (1980) Product or process? A reply to Brian Crittenden, reprinted in J. Rudduck and D. Hopkins (eds) (1985) *Research as a Basis for Teaching* (p. 85). London: Heinemann.
12. Stenhouse, L.A. (1975) op. cit., p. 24.

13. Meece, J.L. (1993) The will to learn (essay review). *Educational Researcher* March, p. 35.
14. Stenhouse, L.A. (1979) Using research means doing research. In H. Dahl, A. Lysne and P. Rand (eds) *Pedagogikkens Sokelys* (p. 75). Oslo: Universitetsforlaget.
15. Stenhouse, L.A. (1979) Research as a basis for teaching. In L.A. Stenhouse (1983) *Authority, Education and Emancipation*, op. cit., p. 163.
16. Ibid, p. 188.
17. Stenhouse, L.A. (1982) Curriculum and the quality of schooling. In L.A. Smith (ed.) *Curriculum and the Teacher*. Proceedings of the Goldsmith's College Education Conference, March, pp. 4–11.
18. Stenhouse, L.A. (1979) Research as a basis for teaching. In L.A. Stenhouse (1983) *Authority, Education and Emancipation*, op. cit., p. 188.
19. Rudduck, J. and Hopkins, D. (1984) *The Sixth Form and Libraries* (p. 117). London: British Library.
20. Harlen, W. (1994) Developing public understanding of education — a role for educational researchers. *British Educational Research Journal*, 20 (1), 1.
21. Stenhouse, L.A. (1979) The teaching of controversial material and the rights of children. In M.L. Van Herreweghe (ed.) *Educational Research in Relation to the Rights of the Child*. World Association for Educational Research, p. 280.
22. Stenhouse, L.A. (1973) *The Humanities Curriculum Project*. Reprinted in L.A. Stenhouse (1983) op. cit., p. 76.
23. Dewey, J. (1938) *Experience and Education*. New York: The Macmillan Company, p. 67.
24. Sarason, S.B. (1991) *The Predictable Failure of Educational Reform*. San Francisco: Jossey Bass, p. 163.
25. Ibid, p. 163.
26. Stenhouse, L.A. (1964) Aims or standards? *Education for Teaching* 64, May; reprinted in L.A. Stenhouse (1983), pp. 48–54.
27. Ibid, p. 49.
28. Ibid, p. 49.
29. Ibid. pp. 53–4.
30. Stenhouse, L.A. (1977) Teachers for all seasons. *British Journal of Teacher Education* 3 (3), 241.
31. Stenhouse, L.A. (1980) Curriculum research and the art of the teacher. *Curriculum*. Reprinted in L.A. Stenhouse (1983) op. cit., p. 161.
32. Stenhouse, L.A. (1977) Teachers for all seasons, *British Journal of Teacher Education*, op. cit., p. 241.
33. Stenhouse, L.A. (1975) The aims of the secondary school. Reprinted in L.A. Stenhouse (1983) op. cit., pp. 153–4.

1 The National Curriculum, School Organisation and the Teacher

BRIAN SIMON

I want to start with a few general, but very personal, impressions. My own engagement with Lawrence Stenhouse — and the very unusual and stimulating team around him with whom, to my mind, he is inseparable — began when Jean Rudduck invited me, at an early BERA conference at Westfield College in London, to act as external examiner for the full-time MA — then the only teaching commitment at the Centre for Applied Research in Education at the University of East Anglia (UEA). This team, from the Humanities Curriculum Project, was of course funded (or, more accurately, I believe, partially funded) specifically as a research unit (in 'Applied Research') at UEA — itself a highly imaginative move masterminded, I believe by Geoffrey Caston; the sort of thing that was still possible in the expansionist mode of the early seventies when some of those in authority were still prepared to search out and encourage imaginative and innovative thinkers and practitioners and, in a sense, to give them their head.

There is perhaps no better way of penetrating into the inner thinking, outlook, emphases, relationships within an educational institution than that of action as external examiner — especially if the students whose work is being evaluated are a relatively small group whose studies can all be made available. Indeed this stint lasted many years since, when it was completed for the full-time MA, a part-time equivalent had been started and I undertook this also. Of course I shall reveal no secrets (indeed, I have none). But though I came from what might be called a progressive and in some respects an innovative institution — the School of Education at the University of Leicester — each time I took the road to Norwich I knew I was entering a different world. Lawrence argues somewhere that the central focus for educational studies must be education itself, its processes and practice — not, for instance, psychology, philosophy, history, sociology, even if all these have something to offer. This approach of Lawrence's may not now sound so original, and this is, perhaps a measure of advance, but at that time

(15 to 20 years ago) to find an MA course which focused so specifically on the schools, their curricula and organisation, and their relations with the external world; on the processes of teaching and learning within the classroom and the schools as a whole; on staff relationships and their influence on procedures, patterns and outlook; and on local authority involvement and its effect — all this was to me, at least, a complete eye-opener and, more than that, extremely refreshing. Not only that, but the new techniques of research and study being developed, many of which arose out of the team's own research studies, and which owed a good deal to the developing 'Illuminative' paradigm (an issue hotly argued, of course), ensured a rigorous research discipline underlying the new investigative approaches. The result can best be described as a new empowerment of the teachers who, of course, formed the large majority of students. The more long-term product, one could reasonably expect and hope for, was the actual improvement of practice — that is, better schools (which is also a fundamental objective of BERA, being written into our constitution).

But it was not only the content of the work and studies actually achieved which was impressive. There was also the question of relationships — particularly among the staff and students — all adult, of course. I can't attempt to define this except perhaps to say that it contained nothing of the *de haut en bas* element not unusual in universities. Relationships were as between equals, involving mutual respect for the different knowledge, experience and expertise of the teachers–students on the one hand, and the teacher–staff on the other. Both, of course, were primarily and fundamentally involved in research activities. In a very real sense these relationships presented a paradigm of what all educational institutions should aspire to.

Perhaps I have said enough to indicate why, as I regularly, for over 12 years, left Leicester for the flat lands to the East I felt a sense of excitement, even of liberation. This achievement was, of course, that of the whole team that originally formed the Centre for Applied Research in Education (CARE), and of their later helpers, several of whom are well known to us here. Indeed the historian of education, interested in networks and their influence, is bound in the long run to trace out the origins and development of the CARE network, now widespread not only in Britain but across the English speaking world generally and elsewhere as well. This network stands for very definite values and procedures; values which, I suggest, accrue an enhanced significance with every year that passes.

This is why, at this particular moment in time, it is especially important to recall, and to consider afresh, the main thrust of Lawrence's teaching and consequent procedures.

But this is a subjective undertaking, and I must immediately add, 'as I understand them'; and I do so diffidently, partly because of my own lack of direct involvement in the curriculum reform movement of the late sixties and later, in which Lawrence played so crucial a role.

What is the position that the schools face today? We have a national curriculum, defined and reinforced by statute — but it is already in disarray. This is based on a subject and on an objectives model — both rejected in no uncertain terms by Lawrence himself in a closely reasoned analysis. Modifications, or various measures introduced or announced over the last year seem to indicate that, perhaps unsurprisingly, the traditional objective of enhancing differentiation is being pursued with some vigour. Then there are the continuous indications of back-tracking as regards the scope of the curriculum — particularly ominous, perhaps, being the official proposal for dropping art, music and physical education from the 14–16 curriculum. There have been other indications that, to meet all sorts of immediate difficulties, the whole concept is to be watered down — and again, in an arbitrary, top-down manner.

There was, or course, originally (I refer to the proposals in the notorious Red Book of July 1987) a great deal of justified scepticism about this whole initiative, and, given the terms in which it was there presented, this is understandable. But we must remember that the concept of a common curriculum for all — or set of structured experiences covering the main fields of knowledge and culture — was a major objective of the whole comprehensive reform movement of the sixties and seventies (and earlier). This movement was primarily concerned to obviate early differentiation between groups of children and their consequent segregation, so in effect shutting off access to fuller life opportunities for considerable proportions of the nation's youth. I well recall the early endeavours (back in the 1950s) to show that a common curriculum within the comprehensive school was a practicable possibility. That was the stage when it was necessary to combat the official ideology that children with different types of mind required basically different forms of education — the great majority being destined for secondary modern schools conceived as schools for working-class children 'whose future employment', as an official Ministry pamphlet put it, 'will not demand any measure of technical skill or knowledge'.[1]

That is why, in the present circumstances, the tendency must be to seize on what is positive, or can be made to be positive, in recent legislation. And why one may have sympathy with Peter Newsam's assessment which, while severely critical of some aspects of this legislation, includes the claim that the national curriculum entitles all children to 'a common set of educational experiences pitched at a high level'. Sir Peter is reported as believing that the establishment of this entitlement is the most important achievement of the eighties.[2]

Now, whatever our criticisms of the thinking, or lack of thinking, behind our national curriculum — of the assessment procedures, of the procedures for 'consultation' relating to programmes of study, of the working parties and all the rest — I believe we should accept Peter Newsam's evaluation of the overall significance of this move. I will not attempt an historical assessment as to why it is that a national curriculum, so defined, was actually written into the Act, nor of the major criticism that it is not in fact 'national' since the Secretary of State's own children and those of the governing elements in our society are specifically exempt. This would take us too far from our immediate concerns. But some credit, at least, must be given to the whole lengthy struggle of teachers and others, against continuous government obduracy, both Labour and Tory, for the single exam at 16. This movement was fuelled with the same concept as that of the early comprehensive pioneers. Whatever their faults and weaknesses, the sections of the 1988 Act relating to the curriculum can be interpreted partly as a culmination of what was, essentially, a healthy movement having the educational interests of the mass of the children at heart.

If we accept this analysis, what follows? The results are bound to be contradictory — but this is the nature of all educational development within a divided society and one which, as recent research by Dr Halsey and others clearly indicates, is becoming increasingly polarised. On the one hand, let's assume that, over time, this entitlement curriculum is in fact provided for all — a big assumption in the circumstances. That would involve a great gain. Let us assume also that the four key stage assessment proposals are also put in place, though here there is certainly room for controversy and battles. If these follow the pattern recommended in the Task Group on Assessment and Testing (TGAT) report, as seems likely, what will be the outcome? The entire school population will emerge from the eleven years of compulsory schooling distributed among each of the ten levels. This distribution, I am advised, is bound to follow the pattern of our old friend the normal or Gauss curve; the majority will be bunched around the mean (say levels 4, 5 and 6, or 5, 6 and 7) — diminishing numbers will be on levels 8, 9 and 10 at the upper end, and 3, 2 and even 1 at the other end. In the words of the now famous anonymous high Department of Education and Science (DES) official in his interview with Stuart Ranson, each will have been educated 'to know their place'.[3]

But will they? Here we can foresee a fundamental contradiction — one which lays hidden motives bare. Do we, or the powers that be, genuinely want to educate everyone to the highest possible level? Or do we want them to be educated 'to know their place' in an increasingly divided and hierarchical society? Here Lawrence, who was seized of this contradiction, had something very significant to say.

The idea is alive, he argued in his 1982 Goldsmith lecture 'of criticism grounded in knowledge provided by the school and of literacy as a gate which lets people into the means of thinking for themselves and becoming critical of our society'.[4] But, he asked, is this entry into critical thinking to be the privilege of an educational oligarchy? Is it being stifled in the state system?

Our system [he said] is notable for being in the power of those who do not commit their own children to it and it is accordingly vulnerable. The powerful still do not favour the cultivation among the lower orders of the scepticism and critical intelligence that is valued among their betters. It is for that reason that they point backwards to basics in the face of the potential of the exciting curricula in literacy and numeracy and knowledge to be found in the recent curriculum movement, in the leading state schools and in the more enlightened private schools.

'The decline in investment and support for public education in this country at the moment', he went on, 'is at many points a vindictive rather than a prudent, economy':

At stake is more than 100 years of adventure beyond the mere basics, a span in which schools have — fitfully no doubt — tried to make people independent thinkers capable of participation in the democratic process and of deciding what the future of their society shall be like. Perhaps a faith in expansion and progress underlay that provision for the citizen. We must now find ways of ensuring that a defensive, and more apprehensive, establishment in the context of a contracting economy does not make a critical education an education reserved for privilege.

These words were not lightly spoken. They form the concluding paragraph of what was, I believe, Lawrence's last public pronouncement in March 1982. They therefore deserve to be taken extremely seriously. Nor were these words, and this judgement, mere rhodomontade — mere rhetoric. On the contrary, this judgement arose out of Lawrence's own final research project, looking, as he put it, at academic sixth forms and the growth of independent study. He found the private schools well equipped, with plenty of money, able to re-form their libraries, to buy more books, to provide everything required for high level study on these lines. At the worst end of the state system, on the other hand, he found sixth form students saying that there are not enough books to go round the class, and that the books there are, are torn and coverless. This, then, was what he called 'the binary divide'. 'There is a real division', he said, 'And I think the division is widening.' But there was, he felt, a deeper reason than mere economy for the conditions he found in the people's schools — the fear of critical thinking, of the potential uses of literacy. It was this fear — of the power of independent thinking — which was the most important factor underlying the parsimony affecting public education. This is what he meant by a 'vindictive, rather than a prudent, economy'.[5]

It follows, surely, that at this clearly crucial moment of change, we need to seize the opportunities with both hands that history has, perhaps unexpectedly, given us. The national curriculum is there on the statute book for whatever reasons. Can we transform it into the 'common set of educational experiences pitched at a high level' which Peter Newsam sees as 'the most important achievement of the eighties'? And in the process of transforming it along these lines, can we not also aim to introduce those modifications which will change it from a top-down, managerially inspired and bureaucratic initiative into a flexible instrument which, while providing the necessary structure to ensure progression, leaves scope for, indeed encourages, local, school, even teacher variation according to the strength and specific characteristics of different traditions, schools and teachers? Such, I suggest, must be the perspective.

And if it is a statutorily based entitlement curriculum, imposed by Act of Parliament, then government has a very clear and specific responsibility to ensure that the legal requirements they have laid down are in fact implemented. Historically, governments in this country have established by Act of Parliament standards relating to school buildings, to safety measures, to school meals, travel and many other matters — for instance, defining the years of compulsory schooling. Now, for whatever reasons, the government has taken it upon itself to define the curriculum in state schools (or most of them) involving the definition of attainment targets, programmes of study and assessment procedures. It remains now the clear responsibility of government to ensure the implementation of these measures in all the schools of the country, both primary and secondary; to provide effectively for the supply of the required number of qualified teachers in each of the defined subjects or subject areas; to ensure the provision of the necessary resources, in terms of books and equipment, for all schools and pupils, since without all these the programmes of study and the national curriculum generally cannot be effectively implemented. As we all know, these are huge tasks, but in fact only part of what needs doing. No previous government in the history of this country has ever undertaken so enormous a responsibility in the field of education. It is surely our job to ensure that the extent of this responsibility, voluntarily undertaken by this government, is fully understood — by the people at large and by the government itself; even if, as Lawrence said in the closing words of his Goldsmith lecture, 'a defensive and more apprehensive establishment' may even now be seeking to ensure that a critical (which requires a full) education is one reserved for privilege. That option must be closed. In drawing attention to the exteme backwardness of this country in education, Sir Claus Moser has, I believe, rendered a public service of great value. Perhaps this will help trigger a national movement for fundamental change in which the full implementation of the national curriculum, modified through discussion and experience, must form a part.

I want at this stage to make a clear and definite assertion. It is that, if we genuinely wish to offer a full entitlement curriculum, or set of common educational experiences, to *all*, this requires, at least at the current historical stage, the full and deliberate implementation of the principle of comprehensive education — and in every area of the country (there are still wide areas, for instance in Kent,

Lincolnshire and elsewhere, where the divided system still holds out, though popular local campaigns are now developing in some of these areas demanding an end to this anomaly). Lawrence himself was highly critical of the previous set-up. 'Historically the great majority of the children of this country', he wrote, 'have been offered in the state educational system, whether through the elementary school or the secondary modern school, no more than a rudimentary education in the basic skills and such an acquaintance with knowledge as might be expected to inculcate a respect for those who are knowledgeable' — this in his inaugural lecture on appointment to his chair at UEA in 1979.[6] Elsewhere, a little earlier, Lawrence made the point that now that the transition to comprehensive secondary education was secure, full attention could and should be turned to the curriculum — since the structural base for the provision of an effective secondary education for all had been achieved. But here, perhaps, there was a certain over-optimism. Can one doubt that, today, the full development of comprehensive education, on the brink of achievement, one might say, in the late seventies, is under threat; that the reinforcement of hierarchic structures within and now also outside local authority systems is in danger of creating a situation which negates the positive aim of providing the crucial common educational experiences for all?

There are many aspects of the Education Act of 1988 which have this tendency, intended or unintended. LMS, open entry, encouragement of increasingly sharp competition among schools for pupils — the whole competitive ethos being deliberately developed will, if full rein is given and taken, inevitably result in winners and losers — and in the losing schools there will be tens, and even hundreds of thousands of pupils (and teachers) who will lose out. That is one threat, or set of threats, but there are others.

The most important of these relate to local government, its status and role. My own earlier analysis of both Bill and Act interpreted it as predominantly an attack on local government, and especially on its historic role in the provision of local systems of both primary and secondary education, and of course also further and higher education. This is too big a question to go into here, but recent events have made it clear to all, surely, that the conflict between central and local government, particularly on financial issues, is increasingly sharp, while from the 'think tanks' of the right increasingly shrill demands are heard proposing the removal of education altogether from local democratic control. Within education — and those areas that most directly concern us — the deliberate down-grading of the responsibilities of local government is expressed through two specific initiatives, both relating to the construction of the government's third tier of schooling: grant maintained schools (GMS) and City Technology Colleges (CTCs). Both directly threaten the stability of local authority 'systems', and, by de-stabilising these, both directly act to destabilise local comprehensive systems. In this sense, then, we cannot now accept that the comprehensive reform — the

condition for effective curriculum renewal having a universalistic ch
is secure.

Both these initiatives are being pursued with a certain steely purpose — politica.
reputations depend on their success. Four separate units have been established
within, or close to, the DES to propagate or administer these developments —
the head of one of them was knighted recently 'for services to education'. By
such means signals are given as to where the real priorities lie. It is well known
that the intention is to persuade the great majority of schools to opt out, and there
is now talk of further legislation to expedite this move.

But, if we make a realistic assessment of the situation, it is difficult not to reach
the conclusion that both these initiatives have run into difficulties.

At the last count I made, in April 1990, only some 32 schools had been given
the go-ahead for grant maintained status (I believe the total is now 44) but the
great bulk of these were escaping reorganisation, amalgamation or closure resulting
from local authorities' perfectly legitimate, indeed necessary attempts to rationalise
provision in a period of demographic decline. Schools originally expected to head
the rush to opt out — successful comprehensive schools in affluent areas — are
conspicuous by their absence, as are schools in the areas of what the media and
others described as the 'loony left'. In fact what has emerged, and clearly, is
an overall loyalty to local authorities and (dare I say it) to the values these embody,
together with a determination to retain local school systems intact and under local
democratic control. Of course we cannot know what the future will bring, and,
as has been made very clear, the financial inducements now being offered,
especially in terms of capital allocations (but also recurrent), are out of all
proportion to those offered to the mass of the schools remaining within local
authority systems. How far this condition can be allowed to continue is, in my
view, highly debatable.

My conclusion is that the competitive, go-it-alone ethos, is far from emerging
as dominant. The traditions of mutual assistance, co-operation, involving decisions
determined by the good of all rather than some — traditions built up in over 100
years of local administration of education — appear to be too powerful to collapse
at a single blow. There is, then, hope for the future, but, to use Tawney's phrase,
it will be as well to keep our pistols primed and our powder dry.

The Secretary of State has recently given the go-ahead for three more CTCs
— in Wandsworth, Telford and Derby; after a novel (in this instance) exercise
in 'consultation' in which, it has been reported, the great bulk of the responses
expressed total opposition to these initiatives largely on the grounds that their
establishment would damagingly threaten local authority systems — that is, local
neighbourhood comprehensive schools. We have seen 'consultation' of this kind

before — relating to the original Bill. One wonders what is achieved by this method of spurning those immediately concerned with such contempt — unless it is to underline publicly just where power lies, through its naked exercise. But it is worth noting, as relevant to my argument, that this initiative also has, to date, run into the sand — the Treasury, apparently, having called a halt owing to the massive and unforeseen drain on the Exchequer. The limit has been set at 20, though plans for all these have not yet been finalised. Industry has been sceptical, preferring to siphon what resources it is prepared to make available to the maintained system generally. Some CTCs have already an unsavoury history — in terms of financial and political skullduggery. But now plans are being cooked up here also for a wide development of CTCs through utilisation of the voluntary-aided category. So here also the future is unclear, and for this reason also we need to keep our powder dry.

In all this, it seems to me, BERA can play a part — or rather its membership. All such initiatives need close monitoring. This must, of course, be done with an open mind in order to discover just precisely what is happening. Educationists, teachers, local and central government officials, politicians, parents — all have a need to know the precise significance of such initiatives both in their own terms and those of the wider system or set of systems of which they form a part. In 1989 Tony Edwards, John Fitz and Geoff Whitty published their research evaluation of another such initiative — the Assisted Places Scheme; to my mind a model of achievement in terms of approach and methodology.[7] Research projects on a similar scale are now under way relating to both the GMS and the CTC initiative. The Economic and Social Research Council (ESRC), and some grant-awarding charities, have a certain autonomy, and funds have been made available. This is certainly a positive feature of the current scene. There is, however, a real danger of prostitution of research where funding is provided by the bodies themselves responsible for the initiatives to be studied. But this raises issues which, if very much BERA's concern, lie far outside the scope of this lecture.

To return to the main argument, these initiatives, however justified their rationale (and this could be a matter for debate), are certainly designed to strike a sharp blow at locally controlled systems of comprehensive education. For those who still hold to the ideals that fuelled this movement since World War II, 'the overriding, simple and clear objective of local authorities', in the words of Lancashire's Chief Education Officer, Andrew Collier, 'is to fund excellent educational opportunities for all the nation's children'. Mr Collier made this point at the conclusion of a speech (to the Society of Education Officers, of which he is currently President) in which he rejected the CTC initiative in particular as 'a criminal waste of money' — a flash of frustrated rage, perhaps, in a committed local administrator seeing so much attention, and resources direct to a few glitzy schools.[8] If I may express my own very carefully considered judgement on both these initiatives, it is that both are politically and educationally irresponsible. Unable to shake comprehensive education by a direct attack, as was attempted at Solihull six years ago, the technique now resorted to is circumvention, and the profference of glittering gifts. *Timeo Danaos et dona ferentes*, as the Trojans rightly assessed a comparable offer long ago: I fear the Greeks even when bringing gifts.

What is the conclusion to all this? It surely must be clear. We need not only still to carry through, complete and further develop the comprehensive transformation (especially and urgently into the 16–19 age range), but also to buttress and armour it against further depredations. This is a clear condition for realisation of the more ultimate aim — that of ensuring, so far as possible equally for all, a common set of educational experiences, and at a high level. To achieve this the teachers, pupils, all concerned must not be having to look over their shoulders all the time to see where the next threat is coming from — they need stability; they need encouragement; they need resources; and they need confidence in their own ability to transform the situation to reach the desired and, dare I say it, agreed objective. This is the task for the future.

I wonder now if you can still bear with me if I move to my penultimate section — the ultimate one is very short. But I would like now to raise some questions in the expectation that they may help us clarify the road to the future, or, more prosaically, our actions over the coming years.

As everyone knows, Lawrence put his faith, if that is the right word, on what he called inquiry-based teaching — in research as the basis for teaching (the title of his inaugural lecture); and in what he called 'action research', where real classrooms, in the charge of teachers, not researchers, are our laboratories. 'The teacher who founds his or her practice of teaching upon research', he said, 'must adopt a research stance to their own practice: it must be provisional and exploratory'.[9] It is this, he argued, that marks him (or her) out as a professional. As an example, he had referred (anonymously) in his lecture to a very dear mutual friend, sadly no longer with us, Margaret Gracie, known at CARE, according to Lawrence, as 'the hypothesis teacher' — 'a tribute', as he puts it, 'to her capacity to stimulate hypothetical thinking within Bruner's social studies curriculum, MAN, a Course of Study'.[10]

The stimulation of hypothetical thinking — teaching as a research-based activity, a process that must be 'provisional' and 'exploratory' — these were Lawrence's objectives, and I think they are objectives we can all embrace. It is this stance, as I understand it, that characterises the reflective teacher — one who submits his or her own practice to a consistent appraisal. To achieve this is surely no easy task, but if we are to empower our youth — to enable them to achieve rationality, to be articulate, tolerant — in short to develop as students, then the teacher's reflective role, action research, a continuous questioning must be the hallmarks of success. So my question is: how far is this possible, indeed practicable, in the new dispensation now coming into being? In short, will the programmes of study, attainment targets, assessment procedures and all the rest, including the built-in school versus school competitive element, create a situation where the teacher–researcher movement cannot survive? I put it starkly in this sense so that the issue is clear. For many of us, I believe, this movement, concerned as it is not only with classroom processes but also those relating to the functioning of the school as a whole, has represented a nodal point of change — a hope for the future. The professionalisation of teachers in this sense must lie at the heart of the educational process as a whole — pointing the way to better schools and to the improvement of practice — BERA's own objective.

May I now, finally, attempt to draw the threads together and in so doing to formulate what might be acceptable as a broadly based platform of advance, as a guideline for the future?

First, then, should we not attempt to secure, or at least to move steadily and clearly towards, a concept, or transformation of the national curriculum along the following lines:

(1)   That it should become a truly *national* curriculum relevant to and applying to everyone, of whatever school, public or private. No rationale has been offered favouring the exemptions now applying, and deliberately written in from the start. I refer here to the so-called independent schools and the CTCs. A national curriculum should and must be truly national.

(2)   That the national curriculum should be transformed to allow greater flexibility — and in particular scope both for innovation (or curriculum development) on the part of teachers, schools, local authorities, if within agreed, demo-cratically determined guidelines. That it should also allow variation in relation to the needs, and specific characteristics, of particular areas, schools and even individuals or groups of teachers working in similar areas.

(3)   That the national curriculum should be conceived in Peter Newsam's terms, as a set of common experiences, and that working groups of teachers and others should be established to identify these experiences, not necessarily tying themselves to the crude subject differentiation which is being established.

Much could, and perhaps should, be said here about assessment and its role. I am not, however, the person to venture into this minefield, so I mention it only to draw attention to this lacuna which others are far better qualified to fill.

I have made three points about the national curriculum, but my second major point concerns organisation. We need, I suggest, actively to support local authorities, not only in defence of their existing school systems, but, more important, in their development. For nothing can or will stand still. Further, local authorities need support in developing their systems as truly comprehensive, providing as far as possible, as Andrew Collier put it, 'excellent educational opportunities for all the nation's children'. This policy certainly requires the use of positive discrimination to compensate for built-in disadvantages, particularly in heavily populated areas. Also schools must be encouraged not so much to compete with each other — even if there may be a place for emulation — as to co-operate together, and of course with parents and local populations, to ensure the best possible provision. A culture of itnernecine strife can hardly be good for education (as was very clearly recognised by the public schools in the late 1930s when a similar situation exploded there due to financial stringency).[11] The second point, then, is the need to ensure stability through support for the development of local comprehensive primary and secondary school systems, now under attack. Success here is a necessity if the first objective, relating to the curriculum and to the quality of teaching and learning, is to be achieved.

And third — as a condition of development, of the improvement of the schools and education generally, there must be an extension of the teacher–researcher movement, which Lawrence saw as the key to the ultimate improvement of the educational process generally. It is, of course, the teachers who carry through the real work of education. They cannot accept the role of 'agents' for the 'delivery' of the curriculum, in Keith Joseph's memorable words. On the contrary, they can and should be the government's allies in the desired creative renewal of the work of education — of teaching and learning. So, perhaps prematurely answering my own question of a few moments ago, the answer I would give is: Yes; teachers can and must continue to play this role, to develop it more widely. In such involvement lies the true hope for the future.

I close with a single comment about Lawrence made by a local teacher who had been on a CARE part-time MA course:

> I used to so love the quality of his mind: the range, the understanding, the subtlety and delicacy of expression made his thinking very beautiful and his kindness and tolerance made *him* very beautiful.[12]

We cannot all be like him, either in his person or in the depth, the subtlety and sharpness of his thinking. But to renew acquaintance with Lawrence is directly to clarify guidelines for the future. In this sense he is still very closely with us.

Notes and references

This paper was The Lawrence Stenhouse Memorial Lecture delivered at the sixteenth annual conference of the British Educational Research Association, Roehampton Institute of Higher Education, 30 August–2 September 1990.

1. *The Nation's Schools* (1945).
2. *Times Educational Supplement* (1989) 12 December.
3. Ranson, Stewart (1984) Towards a tertiary tripartism: New codes of social control and the 17+. In Patricia Broadfoot (ed.) *Selection, Certification and Control*. Lewes, Sussex: Falmer Press, p. 241.
4. Stenhouse, Lawrence (1982) Curriculum and the quality of schooling. In Leslie Smith (ed.) *Curriculum and the Teacher*. London: Goldsmith's College, pp. 10–11.
5. Ibid.
6. Rudduck, Jean and Hopkins, David (1985) *Research as a Basis for Teaching: Readings from the Work of Lawrence Stenhouse*. London: Heinemann Educational, p. 123.
7. Edwards, Tony, Fitz, John and Whitty, Geoff (1989) *The State and Private Education: An Evaluation of the Assisted Places Scheme*. Lewes, Sussex: Falmer Press.
8. *Education*, 26 January 1990.
9. Rudduck and Hopkins, op. cit., p. 126.
10. Ibid. p. 121.
11. See Wallace, Ron (1990) The Act and local authorities. In Michael Flude and Merril Hammer (eds.) *The Educational Reform Act 1988, Its Origins and Implications*. Lewes, Sussex: Falmer Press, pp. 235–6.
12. University of East Anglia, School of Education, *Newsletter* No 1, 1982–3. This publication includes many personal memories of Lawrence Stenhouse, mostly by local teachers.

2 Initial Teacher Education and the Work of Teachers

DONALD McINTYRE

It is my aim in this lecture to explore the implications of making initial teacher education much more the responsibility of practising teachers than it has been in the United Kingdom for almost a century. I believe this to be an appropriate theme for the Lawrence Stenhouse Memorial Lecture not because initial teacher education was one of Lawrence Stenhouse's major areas of interest — so far as I know, it was not — but because teachers' work certainly was. The work of teachers was important to him because he recognised that the quality of school education depends heavily on the way in which teachers' work is conceived by themselves and by others. To him it was important that that work should not be understood as the mere delivery of a curriculum planned elsewhere. 'The teacher's task', he wrote, 'is to help his [or her] pupils gain entry into a commonwealth of knowledge and skills'.[1] In order to undertake this task, teachers in his view had to be educational thinkers who seek to realise their educational ideas in their practice. Furthermore, 'all well-founded curriculum research and development ... rests on the work of teachers. It is not enough that teachers' work should be studied; they need to study it themselves'.[2]

For Lawrence Stenhouse, then, the work of teachers in classrooms was not only *the* important educational activity but also *the* setting in which educational ideas could and should be tested. He considered it supremely important that teachers should construe their work as including the generation, consideration and questioning of educational ideas through investigation of their own classroom practice: 'Curriculum research and development ought to belong to the teacher ...'.[3]

Without seeking to guess what Lawrence Stenhouse himself would have said, I believe that there are close parallels between teachers having a central place in curriculum research and development and teachers having a similarly central place in initial teacher education. As a matter of *fact*, practising teachers tend to exert the most powerful influence in the socialisation of beginning teachers into the work of teachers. As a matter of *policy*, if teachers are to be extended professionals, or even simple professionals, or even if they are simply to have pride in their work, it is surely of considerable importance that they should have substantial control over, and a major responsibility for, the education of entrants to their profession. If, as I claim, teachers do tend to exert the most powerful influence on entrants to the profession, then the betterment of schools depends on that influence being deliberately exerted in the light of teachers' educational thinking and their self-critical reflection on their own practice.

If there is any validity in these parallels, then the obvious next question is why there has not been a spontaneous upsurge of appreciation from educational researchers and teacher educators for the moves taken in recent months by the UK government to give greater responsibility to teachers for initial teacher education. I believe that there are few educational researchers or teacher educators whose thinking has not followed the lead of Lawrence Stenhouse and the movement he set in train for the empowerment of teachers. Why then have we been so reluctant to welcome the government's moves to empower teachers in relation to initial teacher education?

There are of course many reasons, most but not all of which are, in my opinion, good ones. First, many of us who work in higher education faculties or departments of education understandably feel threatened and justifiably feel deeply resentful. We are resentful because the political campaign which has preceded and accompanied the government initiatives has consisted of scurrilous attacks upon us and our work, and has been based on ludicrously irrational arguments, on grossly uninformed accounts of our practice, and on a view of teaching as an activity which does not require thought except about *what* one is teaching. The intellectual quality of the pamphlets, articles and editorials directed against us has been uniformly pitiful; the following excerpt from a *Daily Telegraph* editorial is sadly typical:

> In the 20 years since a postgraduate educational qualification became compulsory for teachers in state schools, the quality of the education in these schools has plummeted. This cannot be a coincidence. The public schools often take bright graduates straight from university and turn them into first-class teachers. In the state sector, however, trainee teachers are subjected to a torrent of largely bogus educational theory . . .[4]

We are right to be angry that all our hard and serious work to improve the quality of education in schools has been so repeatedly, so publicly, so unjustifiably and so squalidly attacked, and that the attack has been sustained on a basis of ideological bigotry and of support from wealthy and powerful interests. Matthew Arnold, an enthusiastic supporter of school-based teacher education, would none the less weep to see how the philistines flourish at the expense of critical thought. We are *right* to be angry, *but* we must be cautious about where we direct our anger.

In particular, it is not clear how far the government's current intiatives are inspired by or informed by the strident voices of the extreme right; both Mr Patten's Circular[5] and the Scottish Office's pilot study[6] leave a great deal open, and could equally well have been guided by wise and informed thinking within their Departments and Her Majesty's Inspectorate.

There are other good reasons why we should not give our unqualified welcome to the government's moves towards more school-based teacher education. Before considering these, however, I want to consider the case *for* such a move.

The Case for School-based Teacher Education

For the prophets of the radical right, the case is a simple, almost self-evident one: one learns how to teach through experience by *practice*: 'Learning how to practise can only come on the job, with time and experience', says Lawlor[7]; 'There is no evidence that the art of teaching can be taught by one person to another', says O'Keeffe[8]; what is needed, says O'Hear,[9] is not the 'spurious and questionable studies' of educational theory, but a 'solid grounding in the real world'.

As nobody here would I think question, they are of course right in their positive emphasis on 'practice': quality in any skilled activity, any craft, any artistic activity, is heavily dependent on practice. In their ignorance, however, these apologists for school-based inititial teacher education undermine their own case by their oversimplification of what is involved in learning to teach. I want to establish the beginnings of a much better case for school-based initial teacher education by examining the inadequacies of this overwhelming concern with 'practice', and by suggesting that each of these inadequacies points us not towards the primarily higher education type of programme to which we are most accustomed, but rather towards a much richer vision of what school-based initial teacher education should involve.

First it is necessary to point out that some of these pamphleteers even fail to understand the notion of learning through practice. The effectiveness of practice, as for example any sports player knows, depends on the very conscious and deliberate practice of desirable ways of doing things: one understands the idea of it, in principle and through examples, and then one repeatedly tries to put the idea into practice, with the help of various kinds of feedback. That is what practising is. But Lawlor, for example, thinks that teaching practice should be just teaching practice. She is pleased to know that 'PGCE courses nowadays do include a substantial element of teaching practice', but is unhappy that, as she perceives it, 'the periods of training in classrooms are chiefly regarded as providing an opportunity for putting educational theory into practice'.[10]

What is alarming is not so much her perception of current practices, nor her objection to educational theory, but rather the fact that she feels no need to offer an alternative: if practice is all-important, and educational theory is no good, what is it that beginning teachers *should* be practising, or putting into practice? Without an answer, purposeful practice becomes directionless 'experience'. As I shall suggest shortly, Lawrence Stenhouse would have had a ready answer.

One of the reasons why beginning teachers need an answer to the question of *what* they should practise is that most of them come only too ready implicitly to supply their own answer as to what they should practise, and many of these answers of their own are, from any informed point of view, not very helpful. Crucially important elements of learning to teach are recognising that one has such preconceptions about teaching and about learning to teach, recognising that these preconceptions are not the same as everyone else's, and questioning and if necessary modifying these preconceptions. This is just one of the many ways in which learning to teach is a great deal more complicated than learning to drive a car or learning to do the Fosbury Flop. Although we still understand relatively little about what is involved in learning to teach, research during the last few years (succinctly reviewed by Calderhead[11]) has given us some understanding of its complexity. There is now a good deal of evidence showing, for example:

- the powerful influence which student-teachers' previously acquired beliefs about teaching and images of teaching exert on their responsiveness to new information, ideas or practices and on their ways of setting about teaching tasks
- the resistance of such preconceived images and beliefs to attempts to change them
- the inappropriateness of many of these preconceptions for effective classroom teaching
- the very great diversity of these preconceived images and beliefs
- the multidimensional nature of learning to teach, with the development of repertoires of teaching strategies, new understandings of children, subjects, schools and educational ideas, the confronting of new concerns and problems, and shifts in attitudes and values, all interacting in very complex ways
- the important affective aspects of learning to teach, especially with very stressful processes of self-exposure and severe threats to self-esteem and self-concepts; and the consequent need for high levels of emotional support for learners combined subtly with challenges to their preconceptions.

It is clear that the notion of 'practice' is quite inadequate to encompass the complex kinds of cognitive and affective developments thus involved in learning to teach. It also seems clear, however, that school-based teacher education should in principle be much better fitted to foster such learning than teacher education based in higher education institutes. The learning is *for* school situations; it is in schools and for schools that repertoires of teaching strategies are needed, that children are there to be understood, that problems have to be solved and dilemmas of values have to be faced.

Furthermore it is in school contexts much more than in lectures or seminars that individual student-teachers' distinctive, powerful and often problematic preconceptions about teaching most clearly emerge and can most readily be confronted on an individual basis. Also, to quote Calderhead,

> Learning to teach is different from other forms of learning in academic life ... Yet many student-teachers appear to enter teacher training without recognising that learning to teach is different from the previous school learning in which they have been engaged, and in consequence find it difficult to adjust to new learning requirements ... in which the analysis of experience and values, for example, may be an important part.[12]

One might predict that these problems would be reduced if the context for learning were more unambiguously different from that of other academic learning.

It may be suggested then that an important part of the case for moving towards school-based teacher education, far from being that learning to teach is simply a matter of practice, is that learning to teach is in any case so complex that we should stop unnecessarily complicating it further by siting it mainly in the alien territory of a higher education institution. That would be my first argument for moving towards school-based initial teacher education.

A second argument for school-based teacher education is related to one particular respect in which the notion of practice as *the* way of learning to teach is especially inadequate: this is the assumption that the learner-teacher can and should accept given ideas or practices as unquestionably appropriate, and that the task is merely to learn to use these ideas or practices. I return in this context to the parallel I drew earlier between the task of initial teacher education and Lawrence Stenhouse's view of the teacher as curriculum researcher and developer. Whether one is discussing curriculum innovation or beginning teachers' learning, the important truth is that there are not, nor could there be, identifiable practices which can be relied upon, irrespective of context or of the particular people involved, to contribute to good and effective teaching: proposed good practices not only have to be practised but also have to be critically tested.

Let me quote Stenhouse's own summary:

> First, I have argued that educational ideas expressed in books are not easily taken into possession by teachers, whereas the expression of ideas as curricular specifications exposes them to testing by teachers and hence establishes an

equality of discourse between the proposer and those who assess his (or her) proposal. The idea is that of an educational science in which each classroom is a laboratory, each teacher a member of the scientific community. There is, of course, no implication as to the origins of the proposal or hypothesis being tested. The originator may be a classroom teacher, a policy-maker or an educational research worker. The crucial point is that the proposal is not to be regarded as an unqualified recommendation but rather as a provisional specification claiming no more than to be worth putting to the test of practice. Such proposals claim to be intelligent rather than correct.[13]

And:

I have argued ... that the uniqueness of each classroom setting implies that any proposal — even at school level — needs to be tested and verified and adapted by each teacher in his [or her] own classroom. The ideal is that the curricular specification should feed a teacher's personal research and development programme through which he [or she] is progressively increasing understanding of his [or her] own work and hence bettering his [or her] teaching.[14]

These ideas of 'translating educational ideas into hypotheses testable in practice', 'the classroom as a laboratory', 'proposals from any origin', 'putting *all* proposals to the test of practice' and 'any proposal needing to be tested and verified and adapted by each teacher in his [or her] own classroom' should, I believe, be at the core of initial teacher education. Included within them, it should be noted, is Lawrence Stenhouse's answer to what should be practised: educational ideas from any origins formulated in terms of hypotheses testable in practice. The tasks of practising new ideas and of testing how far, for what, and in what circumstances these ideas are valuable are necessarily intertwined; and careful collection, examination and analysis of evidence is necessary in order to disentangle them.

Not only is this combined practice and testing of ideas desirable; it is what generally happens in practice. Student-teachers *do* combine their efforts to learn suggested classroom procedures and strategies with their own evaluation of these procedures and strategies as they work in classrooms. What varies is the explicitness, self-awareness and care with which this is done, and the criteria against which proposals are evaluated. Without a good deal of support and help, student-teachers may not make their criteria explicit even to themselves; they may use such criteria as keeping supervisors happy, surviving without unpleasantness, or consistency of new practices with their own idiosyncratic images of good teaching; and they may fail to collect and analyse relevant evidence, to consider implications for other occasions, or generally to make their testing of ideas conscious, systematic and productive. They certainly need a sense of security, of not being overwhelmed by the complexity of the task, by the loss of control, or by the inadequacies of their knowledge. But, just as Lawrence Stenhouse viewed is as a *necessary* condition for curriculum development that experienced teachers should have the commitment, the skills and the opportunity to study their own teaching systematically, so effective initial teacher education is *dependent* on student-teachers not only practising suggested strategies and procedures but also systematically exploring their strengths and limitations.

It is appropriate, I believe, that some of this exploring and testing of ideas for practice should be done within the framework of a professional consensus about what all entrants to the profession should be able to achieve in their classrooms; but that student-teachers themselves should have learned to test, consciously and critically, possible strategies for inclusion in their teaching repertoires is the best guarantee one can have both of their initial competence and of their capacity for continuing development. It need hardly be said that such exploration and testing of classroom strategies, and the support which student-teachers need for doing it, is necessarily school-based.

A third major way in which a view of learning to teach merely through practice is inadequate, not only as a conception of initial teacher education but also in that it sells short the advantages of a school-based approach to teacher education, is its neglect of the expertise of experienced teachers and of what beginning teachers can learn from them. It is true that even the writers of the extreme right tend occasionally to mention 'mentors' who will facilitate and contribute to beginning teachers' teaching practice; but the functions of these mentors seem generally to be limited to making organisational arrangements and passing on some of 'the tricks of the trade — the tips which make for successful teaching' as Lawlor[15] so profoundly puts it. There is not in any of their accounts any sense of the vast body of professional expertise implicit in experienced teachers' practice and which one might hope each generation of teachers would at least in part be able to share with the next.

It is perhaps in this respect that these pamphleteers' views are most profoundly wrong. To a very large degree, the case for moving towards more school-based teacher education should depend on the argument that the people best fitted to educate beginning teachers are those who are already working in the schools; and that the various kinds of arrangements made during most of this century to draw on the expertise of practising teachers for initial teacher education have, even in recent years, been woefully inadequate. But rather than complaining about these mistakes, rather than belabouring us for our failure to recognise and use experienced teachers' expertise and demanding that that be put right, *they* want school-based initial teacher education because they do not believe that teaching requires much expertise; for them, successful schoolteaching depends, like a successful day at the races, on getting and using a few good tips.

We, on the other hand, should recognise both the richness of the teaching expertise used daily in schools, and also the inadequacy of most of our existing organisational arrangements and course rationales in terms of what is done to use this expertise to facilitate beginners' learning. Again, research in recent years has begun to reveal the sophistication of experienced teachers' practical knowledge; the fluency with which it is used; its largely tacit nature; its crucially 'situated' dependence on knowledge about individual pupils, classes and schools; the range of factors of which teachers take account in their everyday classroom decisions; the use they make of previous experiences of situations seen as similar to or contrasted with those confronting them; the individuality of the expertise but its common characteristics. We have learned too that although teachers do not generally in the normal course of affairs make this rich practical knowledge explicit, they can do so in appropriately conducive circumstances.

Even at the simple organisational level, however, the barriers against the effective use of this expertise in initial teacher education have been substantial. Most fundamentally, initial teacher education has necessarily been a marginal activity in schools, not even being one of teachers' statutory duties, and the high-quality time needed for taking it seriously has been available, if at all, in totally inadequate amounts. In addition, teachers have frequently felt their own roles to be both marginal and uncertain in relation to the plans and the teaching of the higher education institutions which have unambiguously had responsibility for the operation; and the relatively brief periods for which student-teachers have generally been in any one school have made sustained facilitation of their development impossible for teachers and have discouraged substantial investment of the schools' energies. It is clear that there is a very great deal of scope for much more effective use of teachers' expertise in initial teacher education.

My conclusion up to this point, then, is the very simple one that a very much better case can be made for a move towards school-based teacher education than has been made by the noisiest proponents of such a move. Beyond that, I hope and believe that we as a professional community of educational researchers and teacher educators can say to Mr Patten, for example, that we understand the potential advantages of such a move very much better than do the pamphleteers of the extreme right; and that if the government wishes its initiatives in that direction to succeed, we are available to talk about them seriously in a way that the pamphleteers have demonstrated they are incapable of doing.

Problems with School-based Initial Teacher Education

The potential of a more school-based approach to initial teacher education is, I have argued, considerable; but I have also suggested that recognition of this has to be complemented by the realisation that such an approach is necessarily quite complex in the understandings and the procedures involved.

Evidence is beginning to accumulate showing that the quality of professional education provided in school-based programmes is in practice likely to be very limited unless the complexity of the task is recognised and steps taken to create the conditions necessary for effective school and teacher involvement. Feiman-Nemser and her colleagues,[16] for example, studied a Californian mentoring programme in which mentors were given much fuller training than has been possible so far in any programme in this country. They were led to ask: '*Are mentor teachers teacher-educators?*' because of the superficiality, unhelpfulness, and especially the lack of challenge of the beginning teachers' practices and pre-conceptions which they found. In Israel, Ben-Peretz and Rumney[17] found that supervising teachers tended in post-lesson conferences to dominate the short conversations that occurred, to evaluate the observed lessons in authoritarian ways, and to mention few alternative possibilities, while the novice teachers played a merely passive role. In this country, Elliott & Calderhead,[18] studying an articled teachers' scheme, found that mentors varied widely in their conceptions of their roles, in the strategies they adopted and in the rationales they held for their activities. The emphasis was frequently on nurturing and on building personal relationships, with images of work with primary school children seeming to exert a strong influence on conceptions of how to work with adult articled teachers. Helping the novices to gain access to craft knowledge was rare, as were conversations in which the novices' preconceptions were challenged.

To be critical of the individual teachers whose mentoring work has been observed in such studies would be to seriously misinterpret the situation; but to encourage moves towards school-based initial teacher education of the kind which these studies reveal would be extremely irresponsible. There are at least three important reasons for believing that, without careful, informed and substantial measures to help schools to prepare themselves for the task, the general picture would be no more encouraging.

First, just as most student-teachers start their professional education with deeply embedded, powerful and stable preconceptons about teaching, so most experienced teachers seem to have similar preconceptions about the process of learning to teach. Very few have ever had any reason to study what is involved in learning to teach, and in normal circumstances few will have the time, the opportunity or the motivation to do so. Yet unless the teachers responsible for school-based initial teacher education develop a much deeper appreciation of the problems of learning to teach, and much fuller understandings of the needs and the possibilities, their efforts may frequently be misguided or superficial.

Second, the task of school-based teacher education is greatly complicated by the nature of teachers' expertise. There are a whole range of problems here.

Given that teachers' expertise is primarily practical, in the sense of being embedded in their practice, the question of how to get access to such expertise is far from trivial. Given that it can be far simpler for teachers to talk in authoritative tones and in terms of generalised maxims about good practice than it is for them to tease out the complex situational considerations which inform their actual practice, the motivation, the patience and the time required to reveal their genuine expertise can be difficult for teachers to find. Given that teachers' expertise consists to a considerable degree in a fluency in lesson preparation and classroom decision-making, dependent on repertoires and skills developed over many years, it is difficult to know what aspects of the expertise are *relevant* for novices who lack such repertoires and skills. Given that the learning needs of novices inevitably vary and change in ways that are difficult to predict, how can it be arranged that teachers' relevant expertise is accessible when it is needed? Given the stylistic and personality differences apparent among both experienced teachers and among novices, how can novices be helped to learn from the expertise of experienced teachers from whom in holistic terms they want to differ?

All these problems associated with the nature of teachers' expertise are, I am confident, soluble; but the more we come to rely on a school-based system, the more essential it will be to take these major problems very seriously.

The third major set of factors which make school-based initial teacher education problematic are those concerned with the quality of schools as professional learning environments. A number of different but probably interrelated factors appear to be important here. Probably most fundamental, and certainly most fully documented, is the dominant cultural norm in most schools of teaching being something personal and private, so that beginning teachers learn, like their more experienced colleagues, to experience the rewards of classroom success and the pain of classroom failure, in isolation. The benefits of collegiality, of the sharing of experiences, reflections, successes and failures with colleagues, have been convincingly argued,[19] and have been dramatically exemplified in the literature,[20] but appear still to be quite rarely experienced.

Along with the expectation that one may talk seriously about one's classroom work with one's colleagues, other cultural norms that would seem necessary to support school-based initial teacher education are a confidence that problems of teaching are likely to be soluble by individual or corporate action, and a related readiness to consider such problems openly and analytically.

Two further aspects of school culture which are of particular importance for initial teacher education have seemed to us especially problematic in our experience in the Oxford Internship Scheme.[21] One of these is the difficulty of breaking through 'the politeness barrier'; interns consistently experience difficulty, even when their relations with their mentors and other teachers are very good, in discussing aspects of the school's or individual teachers' practices which they feel inclined to question: while their learning depends on open discussion of such matters, their junior status and general cultural norms seem to make this kind of questioning inappropriate. (A related difficulty is that of persuading mentors of the appropriateness of them talking critically in conversations with their interns about ideas which the interns have learned in the university department.)

The other problem, of a similar kind, also relates to mentors' discussions with interns about educational ideas and practices. Our evidence suggests that within this initial teacher education context, teachers seem to feel obliged to talk about good practice almost exclusively in terms of what is in the interests of pupils, excluding from their discourse almost any mention of the wide range of practicality criteria which are necessarily of major importance in their own practice. Whether this is because teachers are unconsciously modelling themselves on their experience of how teacher educators behave, or for other reasons, we do not know.

The difficulties of catering for beginning teachers' learning needs within the context of schools' organisations and cultures are well exemplified in a recent paper by Tickle.[22] Most of the beginning teachers he studied had distant and guarded relationships with their mentors, and sought to contain their experiences and learning within the privacy of their own classrooms. Among those with the best relationships with their mentors, help tended to be offered with learning after they had been seen to fail in some respect; and this was not experienced as satisfying or very useful. Ideally they would have liked help in 'being asked the right question' which would create the climate enabling them to reveal their current concerns and thus to get help in *prior theorising* about issues and then to be able to try out useful ideas themselves; but such help was very difficult to get.

I argued earlier that realisation of the very considerable potential of school-based initial teacher education depended on recognition of the complexity of the processes on which that potential depends. I now conclude that the evidence which I have exemplified and the arguments outlined should persuade us that we have hardly begun to understand, far less to develop, the elements of successful school-based teacher education.

Partnership Now and in the Future

In this final section, I therefore want to consider how far and how quickly we should be moving towards school-based programmes, and what kinds of partnership we should be seeking between schools and higher education institutions for initial teacher education.

First, I would suggest that Mr Patten has got three important things right in his Circular.[23] He has got the proportion of time to be spent in schools about right, at two-thirds of PGCE students' time. It allows enough time in school for all the important things which can *only* be done in schools to be done there; and it leaves time in the university for all the things which can equally well be done there. Thus the full potential of school-based teacher education can be explored without arbitrarily shifting activities from universities to schools.

Second, he has got right the decision *not* to have *training schools* that would control and dispense the budgets for initial teacher education, as suggested by David Hargreaves and his co-authors.[24] This is the correct decision because there are some schools whose governors and senior management are arrogant and thoughtless enough to believe they could do the job with little help and little fresh thought; and because, sadly, there are some schools which are in such desperate financial straits that they would divert the money to use it for other purposes; and because, most sadly, there are some schools which are not in serious financial trouble which would still divert the money for other purposes, showing a cynical lack of concern for initial professional education. Mr Patten and his predecessors have released some very destructive market forces in the schools and he is right to guard against them. The partnerships will be better balanced if the schools do not hold all the cards; and experience from the health professions of the exploitation of junior doctors and student nurses by training hospitals offers us a model clearly to be avoided.

Mr Patten is right, thirdly, in that he has specified very little about the structure of, and rationale for, PGCE courses: he has, as I interpret him, put the ball back in our court and left it to us to make the best we can of school-based initial teacher education. It is an opportunity we must grasp with both hands.

What then should be the terms of the partnerships which we should be seeking between schools and higher education? Perhaps the most obvious thing is that the roles should be complementary, and that has major implications for people in higher education: there will be no need whatsoever, in colleges or universities, for people who see their contribution as stemming primarily from their experience and practical wisdom as schoolteachers — that kind of contribution can be supplied much more effectively by *practising* schoolteachers.

Equally, it would be naive and misguided to believe that one of the contributions from higher education should be in training schoolteachers to be mentors. The mentor's expertise is crucially rooted in the school, in knowledge of the school and its culture, in the daily need to face up to the practicalities of teaching, and in the craft knowledge used daily in the cause of education. The new understandings, skills and attitudes that are necessary in order to capitalise on this expertise for the benefit of student-teachers are most unlikely to be in the repertoires of university-based people, or to be adequately understood by us. Where university people are likely to have a major role to play, as Lawrence

Stenhouse would have been the first to see, is in support roles for school staff exploring the possibilities and problems of mentoring. As he said:

> In order to offer support for schools, 'educationists' needs to assume a consultancy role in the fullest sense. They need to see themselves as notionally employed by the teacher, and as accountable to him [or her] . . . academic educationists need to avoid building their own status and personal security on a conviction that they are superior to teachers.[25]

A further temptation in developing a view of the kind of partnership required is that of seeing the school as the place where student-teachers are rightly active and busy, and the university as the place where they can more appropriately reflect on their experiences. This is a great temptation, since universities *are* much better places for adult reflection than schools tend to be. Yet I would suggest that we shall have lost the battle for the soul of school-based teacher education and shall have served our student-teachers very badly if, as mentors and university teachers, we do not help them to develop the skills and habits of reflection, individually and corporately, in *school* contexts. I do not see how it is possible to separate the tasks of developing school-based teacher education and developing reflective schools.

There is no reason why all partnerships should have the same rationale, but it is important that higher education institutions should develop very clear shared understandings with the schools of the distinctive contributions which they can make. One of these distinctive contributions is surely indicated in something I have already quoted from Lawrence Stenhouse:

> . . . educational ideas expressed in books are not easily taken into possession by teachers, whereas the expression of ideas as curricular specifications exposes them to testing by teachers . . . The originator may be a classroom teacher, a policy-maker or an educational research worker.[26]

There is surely a major task to be done in feeding student-teachers a rich and balanced diet of ideas in a form suitable for classroom testing, ideas derived from research, from various kinds of theory, and also from practice elsewhere. In addition, as Lawrence Stenhouse would have agreed, student-teachers need to be helped to learn the many other kinds of criteria and tests, apart from classroom effectiveness, necessary for judging the quality of educational ideas. It is here that higher education staff can, I believe, fulfil an essential and distinctive role.

In the longer term, as schools learn to take responsibility for initial teacher education, it is conceivable that the range of such responsibilities which they can effectively undertake may increase; but I believe that there will always be a major role for higher education institutions, both on the simple grounds of some things being done most efficiently with larger numbers and in purpose-built institutions and, more fundamentally, to ensure that professional education does not become mere professional socialisation. In the meantime, however, for at least the next ten years, there is some extraordinarily interesting work to be done in seeking to realise the potential of largely, but not entirely, school-based initial teacher education.

Finally, I am conscious that, as a teacher educator, I have concerned myself exclusively with the question of what the work of teachers can contribute to initial teacher education. Lawrence Stenhouse would, I believe, have been equally concerned with what a responsibility for initial teacher education could contribute to the work of teachers. So let me finish with two words on this. First, resources are crucial: if teachers are not given the time they need to do this work, then it can easily become merely an extra frustrating burden that they have to carry. Furthermore, teachers in our experience at Oxford feel the need for quite substantial support in the shape of frequent extended visits by their colleagues from higher education to work with them in the schools: it is *not* simply a question of shifting resources from higher education into the schools. Given the resources, however, serious engagement in initial teacher education can be enormously work-enhancing for teachers. After the deskilling effects of so many imposed innovations in recent years, here is an innovation which not only gives enhanced status to classroom teaching expertise, but also encourages teachers themselves to recognise the depth and quality of their expertise, to articulate, share and examine that expertise, and thence to seek to develop that expertise more fully.[27] I think that Lawrence Stenhouse might have approved.

Notes and references

This paper was The Lawrence Stenhouse Memorial Lecture delivered at the eighteenth annual conference of the British Educational Research Association, University of Stirling, 26–29 August 1992.
  1. Stenhouse, L.A. (1975) *An Introduction to Curriculum Research and Development.* London: Heinemann, p. 6.
  2. Ibid, p. 143.
  3. Ibid. p. 142.
  4. *Daily Telegraph* editorial, 11 June 1990.
  5. Circular 9/92, Department for Education, London, 25 June 1992.
  6. Scottish Office Education Depatment (1992) *Guidelines for Teacher Training Courses.*
  7. Lawlor, S. (1990) *Teachers Mistaught.* Policy Study No. 116, Centre for Policy Studies, p. 7.
  8. O'Keefe, D. (1990) Equality and childhood: education and the myths of teacher training. In Graves (ed.) *Initial Teacher Education: Policies and Progress.* London: Kogan Page, p. 92.
  9. O'Hear, A. (1988) *Who Teaches the Teachers?* Research Report No. 10, The Social Affairs Unit, p. 6.
 10. Lawlor, op. cit., p. 24.

11. Calderhead, J. (1991) The nature and growth of knowledge in student learning. *Teaching and Teacher Education* 7 (5/6), 531–6.
12. Ibid, p. 533.
13. Stenhouse, op. cit., p. 143.
14. Ibid, p. 142.
15. Lawlor, op. cit., p. 12.
16. Feiman-Nemser, S., Parker, M. and Zeichner, K. (1992) Are mentor-teachers teacher educators? In D. McIntyre, H. Hagger and M. Wilkin (eds.) *Mentoring: Perspectives on School-based Initial Teacher Education.* London: Kogan Page.
17. Ben-Peretz, M. and Rumney, S. (1991) Professional thinking in guided practice. *Teaching and Teacher Education,* 7 (5/6), 517–30.
18. Elliott, R. and Calderhead, J. (1992) Mentoring for teacher development: possibilities and caveats. In McIntyre *et al.* (eds), op. cit.
19. For example, Little, J.W. (1990) Teachers as colleagues. In A. Leiberman (ed.) *Schools as Collaborative Cultures: Creating the Future Now,* Lewes, Sussex: Falmer Press. Biott, C. and Nias, J. (1992) (eds) *Working and Learning Together for Change.* Milton Keynes: Open University Press.
20. For example, Cole, A.L. (1991) Relationships in the workplace: doing what comes naturally? *Teaching and Teacher Education* 7 (5/6), 415–26.
21. Benton, P. (ed.) (1990) *The Oxford Internship Scheme: Integration and Partnership in Initial Teacher Education.* London: Calouste Gulbenkian Foundation.
22. Tickle, L. (1992) The wish of Odysseus: new teachers' receptiveness to mentoring. In McIntyre *et al.* (eds) op.cit.
23. Circular 9/92, Department of Education, London, 25 June 1992.
24. Beardon, T., Booth, M., Hargreaves, D. and Reiss, M. (1992) *School-Led Initial Teacher Training: The Way Forward,* Cambridge Education Papers, No. 2, Department of Education, University of Cambridge.
25. Stenhouse, L., op. cit., p. 192.
26. Ibid, p. 142.
27. McIntyre, D. and Hagger, H. (1992) Professional development through the Oxford Internship Model. *British Journal of Educational Studies* XXXX, (3), 264–83.

3 Uncertain Knowledge and Indeterminate Practice

TONY EDWARDS

There is some irony in this occasion, because I take it that lecturing is not an activity of which Lawrence Stenhouse approved. I have tried to recognise that by offering some appropriately non-authoritative thoughts on our present condition, prompted by his exploration of the uncertainty of research knowledge and school knowledge, and of consequences for educational practice which follow from that uncertainty.

The lecture's title also suggests roots in Daniel Schön's analysis of reflective practice and of how reflective practitioners might be educated. The roots are shallower than I expected when I thought of the title long before thinking about the talk, and I hope my attempt to fit the two together will not seem contrived. But Schön's account of professional 'artistry' has obvious relevance to recent assertions, too systematic not be a campaign, that educational theory is a pretentious and propagandist distraction from the real task of learning to teach by emulating and being supervised by masters of the craft. For if that campaign were ever to move beyond caricaturing its target, it could make use of his celebration of 'the competence already embedded in skilful practice'; his scepticism about the rational application of technical knowledge to practical problems; and his advocacy of coaching. Of course the borrowing would have to be selective. Attacks on teacher educaton tend to treat effective teaching as an unproblematic passing on (or passing down) of what the teacher knows about — a simple consequence, given practice, of 'knowledge and love of subject'. Schön emphasises the complex, problematic nature of professional practice; its skills should be reflected upon and investigated, not taken for granted, and the explicit questioning of established methods is strongly encouraged. 'Applied science' is part of those processes, provided it is brought down from the high ground where 'relatively unimportant problems' can be solved according to 'prevailing standards of rigour' and directed instead towards the important problems which only arise in 'messy, indeterminate situations'. Where their critics deny that 'educationists' have any useful knowledge to offer, even assuming that classroom problems could be solved

44

by applying what has been learned elsewhere, Schön suggests that the dilemma of 'rigour or relevance' in professional education should be resolved by teaching the 'science' as a mode of inquiry.[1]

By now I hope that links with the work of Lawrence Stenhouse are apparent. He was critical of 'book learning about education' which was not 'disciplined by the problems of practice', especially when it displayed an undemocratic tendency to make research a mystery penetrable only by insiders. He wished to empower teachers against external 'experts', seeing the surest foundation for professional autonomy as a trained capacity for investigating and reflecting on their own practice. But other lecturers in this series have been far better fitted to build on his commitment to action research as a means to educational improvement. My own thinking has been prompted by his exploration of how knowledge should be used, both research knowledge and school knowledge, in circumstances marked (in Schön's phrase) by 'uncertainty, uniqueness, and value conflict'.

Unlike others who have given the Memorial Lecture, I knew Lawrence only slightly. Our last meeting was at a workshop for classroom researchers which Bob Burgess organised. Although it was only a few months before his death, his vitality in argument was undiminished. No doubt it reflected his sympathy with the purpose of the discussions, which was to examine those false starts, blind alleys and mistaken choices which are so often tidied out of research accounts.[2] For he rejected any notion of research as yielding 'established authoritative knowledge', uncritical appeals to 'what research has shown' being no more acceptable than any other form of unquestioning belief. He therefore also rejected entirely Ben-David's proposition that 'knowledge that can be taught no longer needs to be investigated, while knowledge which still needs to be investigated cannot yet be taught'. On the contrary, he argued, what is taught in universities should be presented as being in some sense provisional, the best we know at present, open to further investigation. Such knowledge cannot then be 'taught correctly except through some form of research-based teaching' because it is fatally flawed by being separated from the processes for enquiry which are its warrant. Those teaching it must be aware, through their own experience of investigating some small part of their field, of the uncertainties that abound.[3] As the next research selectivity exercise begins to take shape, it will be worth recalling that powerful argument against separating the production of knowledge from its transmission. There is a view that while 'scholarship' is a necessary foundation for teaching in higher education, research is not. Lawrence Stenhouse would have firmly rejected that distinction.

I want to argue that his challenge to knowledge justified by appeals to authority has particular contemporary relevance to education. The highest status has been given to that systematic, preferably scientific, 'knowledge' which is developed on the high ground and then brought down and put to work. Educational research has usually been placed on the lower slopes. Occasionally, as I commented years ago on the largely uncritical acceptance of Berstein's explanation for working-class educational failure, an education profession unpractised in taking research seriously may occasionally for that reason take it too seriously. Far more often, research findings which seem useful to policy-makers and opinion-makers are taken up and vigorously sponsored in expediently edited form. 'Ministers trawl the Leeds report', said *The Times Educational Supplement* (16 August 1991), 'to see what wisdom it offers them for their Citizen's Charter', and Robin Alexander has already complained of his report's misuse by those wishing to attack local education authority 'dictation', the 'folly' of egalitarian interventions, and (of course) the 'failure' of 'progressive' approaches. In fairness I should add that if we believe Caroline Cox and John Marks, inconvenient findings have been much more at risk of being stifled or travestied and discredited by the 'liberal establishment', including that part of it entrenched in and around the Department of Education and Science (DES).[4]

It may be better to be noticed unfavourably than to be ignored, but educational researchers hope for more positive recognition. The usual pressures, temptations and inclinations to be useful have been intensified by the various 'natural experiments' created by the government's reforming zeal, and by a wish to counter criticisms of educational 'theory' as being subversive where it is not merely unhelpful. Indeed, a commitment to useful service is, understandably and properly, the theme of this conference. There is, however, the other inseparable task which Robert Lynd identified in answering his own question about the social sciences: 'Knowledge for what?'; it is the obligation to 'be troublesome, to disconcert the habitual arrangements by which we manage to live along, and to demonstrate the possibility of change'.[5]

Lynd was not advocating the role of detached and perpetual critic, the kind of oppositional stance which Sally Brown warned against at last year's BERA. If the social sciences were obliged to be troublesome, they were also 'instruments' for 'coping with areas of strain and uncertainty'. If so, they are badly needed as the pace of educational change creates increasing strain and uncertainty. But the responsibility of educational researchers to help make reforms succeed is not fulfilled by assisting without good cause in the creation of certainty. I refer not to the increasing tendency for research funding to seek readily usable, convenient, answers to policy-defined questions, important though that tendency is, but to the surely unusual extent to which educational 'facts' are simply affirmed, and enquiry into them denied or delimited or prematurely closed. Opponents of the 'educational establishment' would argue that what is new is not the appeal to ideology but the values to which appeal is made, complaints merely reflecting the chagrin of 'egalitarian progressives' who no longer have everything their own way. But even in the heyday of that establishment, I doubt if education was so plagued by certainties.

'The Tory will abhor the theory that tells all', and will 'deplore the politics of the simple answer'. There is some pleasure in identifying the present Chairman of the party as the source of those instructions, but unfortunately they have not been followed.[6] We will all have our own selection of simple answers to complex educational problems, but the obvious contender for the theory that tells all has been a faith in the beneficient effects of market forces. Mary Warnock has commented on how previously dominant metaphors drawn from the garden and the greenhouse have been replaced by a language of utility, saleability and cost-effectiveness drawn from the shop and the marketplace.[7] That language has expressed the conviction that the 'free' interplay of supply and demand, and the consequent competition between schools obliged to provide 'hard' evidence of their quality, guarantees higher educational standards. It was the recent claim of American researchers, eagerly publicised, that 'choice *is* a panacea' (the emphasis is theirs). Even allowing for the different contexts, it is worth contrasting their conclusion that (for example) 'under-enrolment is simply a bureaucratic euphemism for what happens when schools are so bad no one want to attend them' with the rigorous analysis by Michael Adler and his colleagues at Edinburgh of the complex interaction of individual rights with collective interests in the exercise of choice, and their conclusion that the accumulated effects of 'free' parental choice may be to increase educational inequalities and sharpen social divisions.[8] As for the information about schools' comparative performance to which individual consumers should have access, the highly technical debate about 'raw' and 'cooked' data takes place in a highly politicised forum in which the dominant political assumption is that 'rawness' is healthier. Despite its rather ominous title, the National Consortium for Examination Results is to be commended for its dedication (according to its Secretary) to providing evidence that 'DES theories about publishing examination results . . . won't work'.[9] It is too tempting at this point not to offer another quotation made appealing by its source. 'A performance indicator is a number which can be calculated by a good statistician without any exercise of judgement, and which is seen as a surrogate for what one is actually interested in'. In his Rede Lecture in May this year, shortly before his leaving the Universities' Funding Council, Sir Peter Swinnerton-Dyer went on to regret that 'Unfortunately, outsiders are apt to believe they provide an adequate means of assessing a system without the labour of understanding it.'

I am reminded of Lawrence Stenhouse's scepticism about how far worthwhile knowledge and understanding 'can be expressed in terms of specifiable and common student behaviours', and about output models of educational peformance which 'assume a capacity to predict results of curricula which is not justified by empirical work'.[10] At least from that perspective, I have sympathy with Lord Griffiths' question about the TGAT[11] assessment structure which (as SEAC's[12] new chairman) he clearly intends to simplify. 'Where', he asked, 'do we have evidence of success in this kind of approach before?'[13] But it is the general point, and not that salient example, which I want to emphasise. Researchers have an especially heavy responsibility in the present climate of politically expedient and doctrinaire simplifications, to say loudly when 'we do not know', or 'we do not know enough', or 'it really is more complicated than that'. When so many assertions about how things 'are' in the schools are derivations from ideology which avoid the labour of looking, there is some irony in the blame bestowed on 'educationists' and 'shadowy experts' for uncritical propagation of fads and fashions. That 'the sleep of reason brings forth monsters' was a text for the Black Paper sermons against the 'progressive fallacy'; the monsters are no less monstrous for entering Stage Right.

When the warning was used to preface counter-attacks against the 'progressive consensus', the Humanities Curriculum Project was attached to that supposed 'establishment'. Indeed, I had to check whether it had been included in the lists of infamy (which it was not), and whether Lawrence Stenhouse himself had been numbered among the perpetrators of 'progressive collapse' (which he was not, though Brian Simon was).[14] The Project was certainly perceived 'in the climate of the time' (Lawrence noted) as being child-centred, informal and anti-intellectual, because that was what any authorised innovation was then expected to be. What it actually was, however, illustrates the folly of easy polarities and over-sharpened contrasts. Prominent in the hagiography of 'progressivism' have been a preference for 'understanding over knowledge', a liking for 'feeble empathising with the power orders of the past', a deference to the 'distracting slogans of relevance' a distaste for 'tedious facts' and any tasks not immediately palatable to the learner, and an enjoyment of splashing around in 'an amorphous tide of easy-going discussion' and 'opinionated vagueness'.[15] Yet the Humanities Project was explicitly knowledge-centred. Quite unlike that emphasis on what is easy and 'relevant' which is routinely attributed to integrated studies by defenders of 'real' subjects, the knowledge came from topics of 'enduring human interest', and 'relevant to our cultural tradition'. They were topics which those in the last years of compulsory schooling 'ought' to explore in depth. Nor were they a replacement for subjects, the different logics of which he believed should be respected. The whole enterprise was explicitly intellectual in approach.

I have had to be tactically selective in outlining such apparently common ground, because the neo-conservative Right wants 'proper' subjects to be authoritatively taught. Here a polarising of positions is unavoidable. That relationship of research-based knowledge to teaching which Stenhouse described (and prescribed) for universities, he saw as being entirely relevant to schools. In both settings, the warrant for much of what is taught should be 'rational justification in the light of evidence' and not an appeal to the personal authority of the teacher. Yet classroom research suggests strongly that most teachers teach most things authoritatively. The very unequal communicative rights created and sustained by the transmission of knowledge both reflect and reproduce a clear boundary between those who 'know' and those who do not, and both teacher and students interact as though the knowledge being transmitted is certain and secure.[16]

For his recognition of the strength of the didactic tradition, and of the sense of security which teachers gained from working within that instructional framework, came Stenhouse's commitment to supporting teachers who wished to work in other ways — by producing resources which would free them from some of the constraints of being providers of information, and by defining and demonstrating the strategy appropriate to teaching issues marked by uncertainty and value conflict.

Although any kind of recipe would be entirely alien to his approach, I will briefly illustrate, in the form of advice to the teacher, the extent to which that strategy departs from normal practice. Avoid questions to which you evidently know the answers, because they divert students' attention from the evidence and from any emerging argument to whatever cues and clues are contained in how you respond to what they say. Avoid leading questions, especially those designed to elicit a particular approach to the evidence (which will not speak for itself, but which should not speak simply through you). Encourage students to ask questions. Do not reward contributions in line with your own views. Do not interrupt, have the nerve to accept long pauses and the nerve not to feel responsible for ending them. Avoid turning tasks into guessing games, and do not strive for consensus. I have described the strategy as explicitly intellectual. It is a view of teaching which he justified by argument and evidence, not by exhortation, and he described it with a clear view of the technical difficulties and moral dilemmas which it created for the practitioner. It is also, deliberately, 'rather formal' — an attempt to contain the teacher's authority within clear procedural rules. 'If we conceive of authoritarianism as arbitrary use of authority,' he argued, 'then informal relations readily favour it. In informality, the power of the superior is unbounded.' There are echoes here of Willard Waller's definition of teaching as 'institutionalised leadership' which gains from 'a clear demarcation of boundary lines' and from 'straining' a potentially overpowering personal influence 'through the sieve of formality'.[17]

The non-authoritative strategy was developed for a particular curriculum, but also as a more general challenge to 'normal' teaching. I want now to comment on that challenge in ways which reflect my own past and present research interests. I have long disagreed with Basil Bernstein about the 'underlying semantic' from which pedagogical discourse is typically constructed. If school knowledge is detached from students' everyday experience, it also tends to be protected from critical scrutiny. The common outcome is a 'non-reflexive relationship to bodies of knowledge which are already established, and which are there to be received and displayed but not challenged'.[18] It is distinctly uncommon to find students being given access to the grounds for knowing what they are supposed to know— the access which Lawrence Stenhouse argued should not be restricted (where it is available at all) to those being sponsored for membership of an occupational elite. For something like a non-authoritative pedagogy is most readily associated (on uncertain evidence) with university seminars, traditional sixth forms in their somewhat mythical guise as the stage at which pupils become students or (in Crowther's phrase) 'intellectual disciples', and with 'leading' selective (and now largely private) secondary schools. And it is a familiar argument that the education system has discouraged, some would argue should discourage, a questioning stance except in those intended for positions of power and authority, variations on rote learning being held sufficient for those for whom routine and subordination to the decisions of others will be basic facts of working life.

The perceived demands of an advanced industrial society, however, have produced significant departures from that view. I invite you to place in their context the following statements of pedagogic aspiration.

A range of learning support services will 'concentrate responsibility for learning on the student', the teacher organising the conditions for that learning rather than 'controlling the rate of it from the front of the class'. The task of devising 'flexible and responsive learning styles' recognises the 'importance of doing and understanding as well as knowing'. 'Learning to study independently' is critical in secondary education because students should leave with the ability to find information and use it objectively; they should know 'how to discriminate and how to assess the value of the information they have accumulated'.

Those statements are taken from prospectuses of the city technology colleges in Bradford and Corby, presenting themselves as offering a distinctively 'modern' version of secondary education. But it is also a version which contains significant ingredients of the 'progressivism' so deplored from the neo-conservative Right. In so far as it is possible to refer to a 'CTC[19] movement', there is a well-publicised determination to cross conventional curriculum boundaries, encourage collaborative investigation and real problem-solving, and produce a radical shift 'from teaching to learning'. Although all this can be justified as an economically useful modernism, a reflection of the very differently skilled workforce which employers now see as needed, it bears some resemblance to Stenhouse's emphasis on 'mastery of seeking' rather than on 'mastery of knowing'. From that perspective, it will be interesting to see (for example) how far the CTCs' high investment in information independently of the teacher's mediation, and how far it reinforces the authority of packaged knowledge with the prestige of Caxton's electronic suburbs.

From a broader perspective, however, that interest would seem esoteric. For whereas Stenhouse argued for non-authoritative teaching as a democractic strategy, the emergence of CTCs is one expression of a commitment to greater choice and diversity which threatens a much sharper layering of educational provision in relation to both curriculum and pedagogy. It is with this threat that I want to end. Now with similar reservations about its origins and implementation, and about its often arbitrary reshaping, I share the view which Brian Simon expressed in the 1990 Memorial Lecture — that the national curriculum offers, potentially, a higher common level of knowledge and understanding than has been offered in the past. It might be argued, in Bernstein's terms, that if middle-class students are most advantaged by the weak marking of content and sequence, then some equalising effects could be expected from the highly visible pedagogy embodied in statutory requirements and non-statutory guidance — a framework of authoritatively defined knowledge, strong rules for sequencing and pacing it, and the grading of its acquirers against explicit external criteria.

But that expectation is too abstracted from reality to be consoling. During the past year, there has been a marked narrowing of the 'broad and balanced' curriculum initially promised. The government is sponsoring a back-to-basics approach for inner-city children which can be defended as a necessary foundation for more advanced study, and attacked as a meagre alternative to it. The Secretary of State has been peremptory in expressing some of his curriculum preferences, and unreasonable in the pace at which complicated revisions of attainment targets are required. And writing to SEAC earlier this year [1991], he defined the purpose of national tests as being to provide 'a rigorous and objective measure of pupils' attainments', and not to 'promote particular approaches to the delivery of the curriculum'. That is surely disingenuous. Practice is powerfully shaped if well-marked priority is given to 'certain' knowledge and 'readily' measureable skills, and examinations are a familiar mechanism for reshaping teaching — hence the fierceness of attacks from the Right on GCSE and the accompanying preference for 'proper' examinations over an extensive national curriculum as a means of control. The misuse of pupils to monitor schools and keep teachers up to the mark, as Mary Warnock put it,[20] creates very high-stakes testing indeed — especially in increasingly competitive conditions where the consequence of failure is intended to be a 'deserved' loss of custom and so of resources. The pressures likely to squeeze out less authoritative, more demanding and more emancipating forms of teaching will be strongest in those schools already working in the most difficult conditions and likely to be losers in a new market economy of schooling. They will be the schools least able to take risks. The outcome could be a system rigidly stratified not only in relation to anything resembling a broad and balanced curriculum. It could also be stratified in relation to how far the curriculum being offered is seen as being simply 'delivered'.

It is the context of that warning, not I hope a prediction, that I want to end appropriately with Lawrence Stenhouse's words. He was contemptuous of that 'ideological parsimony' which seeks to restrict the inclination and capacity to explore the grounds for what we know, and to make it 'an education reserved for privilege'. If schooling should be 'a gate which lets people into the means of thinking for themselves', then it should be a broad gate and a broad highway'.[21]

Notes and references

This paper was The Lawrence Stenhouse Memorial Lectured delivered at the seventeenth annual conference of the British Educational Research Association, Nottingham Polytechnic, 28–31 August 1991.
1. Schön, Donald (1987) *Educating the Reflective Practitioner*. San Francisco and Oxford: Jossey-Bass.
2. That workshop, and its predecessor, are recorded in R. Burgess (ed.) (1985) *Field Methods in the Study of Education*. Lewes, Sussex: Falmer Press; and in R. Burgess (ed.) (1984) *The Research Process in Educational Settings: Ten Case Studies*. Lewes, Sussex: Falmer Press.
3. Stenhouse, L. (1983) Research as a basis for teaching. In L. Stenhouse *Authority, Education and Emancipation*. London: Heinemann Educational. This was his inaugural lecture given in 1979 as Professor at the University of East Anglia.
4. Cox, Caroline and Marks, John (1988) *The Insolence of Office*. London: Claridge Press. Their case is taken up by Hans Esysenck in the summer 1991 issue of the *Oxford Review of Education*.
5. Lynd, Robert (1939) *Knowledge for What?* Princeton: Princeton University Press, pp. 114 and 181.
6. Patten, C. (1983) *The Tory Case*. London: Longman, pp. 31 and 104.
7. Warnock, Mary (1991) Equality fifteen years on. *Oxford Review of Education*, 17 (2), 145.
8. Chubb, J. and Moe, T. (1990) Choice *is* a panacea. *Brookings Review,* summer, 4–12. The evidence, and assumptions, on which that claim is based is reported in their 1990 book *Politics, Markets and America's Schools*. Washington: Brookings Institute. A very different account is presented in Adler, Michael, Petch, Alison, and Tweedie, Jack (1989) *Parental Choice and Educational Policy*. Edinburgh: Edinburgh University Press.
9. *Times Educational Supplement*, 23 August 1991.
10. Stenhouse, L. (1983) *Authority, Education and Emancipation*, op cit.
11. Task Group on Assessment and Testing (1987) *A Report* (The TGAT Report). London: DES.
12. SEAC — the Schools' Examination and Assessment Council.
13. Interviewed by Ian Nash for the *Times Educational Supplement*, 26 July 1991.
14. There is an interesting retrospective view of what the Black Papers achieved in C.B. Cox (1982) Progressive collapse: The counter revolution in English education. *Quadrant* 26 (3), 20–8.

15. The various sources for these denunciations are: The Hillgate Group (1987) *The Reform of British Education*. London: Claridge Press; O'Hear, A. (1987) The importance of traditional learning. *British Journal of Educational Studies*, 35, 2, 102–14; Norcross, Lawrence (1990) The egalitarian fallacy. In *GCSE*. Warlingham: Institute of Economic Affairs Education Unit; O'Keefe, D. (1990) Equality and childhood:: Education and the myths of teacher training. In Graves, N. (ed.) *Initial Teacher Education: Policies and Progress* pp. 74–92. London: Kogan Page.

16. Empirical support for these generalisations is offered in Edwards, A. and Furlong, J. (1978) *The Language of Teaching*. London: Heinemann Educational Books; and in Edwards, A. and Westgate, D. (1987) *Investigating Classroom Talk*. Lewes: Falmer Press.

17. Stenhouse, L. (1983) op. cit., p. 70; and Waller, W. (1932) *The Sociology of Teaching*. New York: John Wiley, pp. 189–96.

18. Edwards, A. (1987) Language codes and classroom practice. *Oxford Review of Education* 13 (3), 237–47.

19. CTC–City Technology College.

20. Warnock, Mary (1988) *A Common Policy for Education*. Oxford: Oxford University Press, pp. 101–2.

21. Stenhouse, L. (1982) Curriculum and the quality of schooling. In Leslie Smith (ed.) *Curriculum and the Teacher* (pp. 10–11). London: Goldsmith's College.

4 Education in the Shadow of the Education Reform Act

JOHN ELLIOTT

Lawrence Stenhouse spent a great deal of his professional life attacking the intrusion of 'technical rationality' into curriculum planning. In the late 1960s this view of practical reasoning appeared in the guise of 'rational curriculum planning'. Curriculum planning, it was argued,[1] could only be rational if it were guided by quite clear and specific statements of intended learning outcomes, defined in terms of measurable changes in student behaviour. Rational planning proceeds by breaking down general aims into more tangible objectives and then selecting learning experiences to achieve them. The assumptions about rationality which underpinned this planning model were as follows:

- questions about the ends of human activities can be separated from questions about how to realise them
- the value of human activities resides in their instrumental (or technical) effectiveness in bringing about desirable outcomes which are extrinsic to the activities themselves. Extrinsic outcomes alone justify the means
- human activities can be justified only if their outcomes refer to observable changes
- rational action proceeds from a prior process of instrumental (technical) reasoning about how to achieve tangible results.

Stenhouse claimed that 'the objectives model' of curriculum planning was anti-educational, and proposed an alternative: 'the process model'.[2] He drew inspiration from the work of R. S. Peters, who by the 1960s had turned his considerable talents and energies to the task of elucidating the nature of education. According to Peters our everyday discourse about the aims of education does not assume that we are talking about the extrinsic outcomes of a process.[3] Rather, Peters argued, we are referring to values and principles which constitute a process as an *educational* one. 'Aims' in educational discourse referred to procedural criteria or principles which were realised *in* rather than *as a result of* the process of education. Stenhouse developed his 'process model' on this 'insight'. Recently I argued that such an 'insight' was actually embodied in the curriculum reform practices of many teachers in secondary modern schools during the 1960s.[4] What Peters and Stenhouse did was to articulate a logic, an alternative form of practical rationality, that was already implicit in the practices of innovatory teachers. I shall explore the implications of this point for curriculum planning at the end of the paper.

Stenhouse's great contribution was to design the Humanities Curriculum Project[5] as an illustration of the radical contrast between the 'process' and 'objectives' models.[5] He began, not with the question 'what are the objectives of the curriculum?', but with a problem-situation that faced teachers attempting to make the secondary school curriculum of the 1960s more relevant to the lives of young adolescents. The problem was 'how do teachers handle value-issues in classrooms within a pluralistic democracy'?

He ruled out two answers to the problem.[6] Firstly, he argued that if education was to be a preparation for life, value-issues should be part of the explicit content of the curriculum. This view in itself sanctioned innovation since the curriculum in all schools largely reflected the academic curriculum of the grammar schools. It was largely subject-based and exclusively concerned with the transmission of factual information. The values implicit in the selection of facts and the human purposes they served were not generally brought to the surface and discussed. Secondly, Stenhouse ruled out the possibility that teachers should use their authority position to promote their own personal commitments. He argued that this was inconsistent with the democratic rights of parents and communities not to have the values they subscribed to undermined by teachers who were committed to different value-positions.

So Stenhouse ruled out two responses to the problem. In doing so he ruled out two kinds of aim: the acquisition of knowledge detached from consideration of questions of value, and the inculcation of a particular value-position. This allowed a third alternative solution to emerge: namely, that students should develop their understanding of human actions and situations in the light of the controversial value-issues they raised. This aim specifies a learning process rather than an extrinsic outcome of learning. Stenhouse refused to specify what the outcome of the process would consist of, but argued that it implied a set of procedural principles. Firstly, that controversial issues should form part of the content of the curriculum in schools. Secondly, that discussion of issues rather than didactic instruction should constitute the core of the classroom process. Thirdly, that teachers should refrain from using classrooms as a platform for promoting their views. Fourthly, that divergence in discussion should be protected. Fifthly, that teachers had responsibility for the critical standards employed in the discussion, e.g. ensuring that views and arguments were tested against standards of reasoning and evidence.

The Humanities Project was designed as a specification of a worthwhile 'educational' process of teaching and learning about value-issues, without determining precisely what the outcomes would be. It was presumed that these would constitute divergent interpretations of controversial human acts and situations, grounded in different value-positions. What such a process does is provide students with opportunities to modify and reconstruct their values in the light of alternative perspectives.

Underpinning the 'process model' is a totally different logic of reasoning to that of technical rationality, namely:

- questions about ends cannot be separated from questions about means
- the value of human activities lies in their intrinsic qualities. Ends justify means because they specify qualities realised in the activities (processes) themselves. They are not extrinsically related outcomes
- activities are justified by their intrinsic ends, and these do not refer to observable effects. They are justified, not on the basis of observable effects, but on the basis of judgemental inferences about the manner in which they are performed
- rational action proceeds from practical deliberation about how to realise ends-in-view *in* concrete activities within particular complex situations. Such ends-in-view cannot be operationally defined in terms of the means they are consituted by in advance of the situation. Means are determined in situ, and therefore always involve an element of 'shooting in the dark'. There is a sense in which the ends are operationally defined through the selection of the means to realise them. In abstract form they remain essentially vague. If asked for operational definitions one can only cite concrete instances of their realisation in particular circumstances. Ends are therefore only clarified by reflection on the experience of particular attempts to realise them in action. In selecting means people also operationally define their ends-in-view. Practical deliberation involves reflecting about means and ends together.

In his *Ethics* Aristotle argued for a distinction between activities which constitute the *making* of a product and those which involve *doing* something well.[7] Technical rationality, or *techne* as he called it, is the form of reasoning appropriate to the making of products, while practical deliberation, or *phronesis*, is the form of reasoning appropriate to doing something well. These two forms of rationality underpinning the 'objectives' and 'process' models of curriculum planning have been around a long time. What Stenhouse objected to was the encroachment of technical rationality into our thinking about education, and its transformation from a practice in the Aristotelian sense of the term to a technology.

Stenhouse died in 1982. What would he make of the Education Reform Act as it casts its shadow across the educational landscape? Professor Brian Simon, in his passionate critique of the 'reforms' at last year's BERA conference, suggested that Stenhouse was surely 'turning in his grave' over a Bill that so clearly undermined his life's work. I cannot predict his response. Of one thing I am sure, it would be an unusually creative and unpredictable one, appropriate to a man once described by David Jenkins as 'a chess player in a world of draughts'.

All we can do is to draw on the legacy of Stenhouse's ideas in formulating our response to the Education Reform Act. This is not simply a matter of applying his ideas to the Act. These ideas were essentially developed as a critical response to the problems and issues posed by the curriculum reform movement of the late 1960s and 1970s. What is required now is a critical response to the problems and issues of the late 1980s and 1990s. Stenhouse's legacy was to draw on a tradition of thinking about social practices, like education, which goes back as far as Aristotle. This tradition is increasingly being drawn on by philosophers and social theorists who feel that the encroachment of technical rationality into every area of social life is endangering fundamental human values. In trying to discern what is at stake in our response to the Education Reform Act we may need to draw even more extensively on the Aristotelian tradition than Stenhouse did. This does not mean that we have to read Aristotle. Stenhouse, to my knowledge, never cited him. Nor did he cite Gadamer[8] who reconstructed Aristotle's thought as a basis for critique of technical rationality. One can secure access to a tradition as a resource for one's thinking without being able to locate the source of the ideas it embodies. Traditions of thought are embedded in our culture. Moreover, they are dynamic, evolving historically as they are applied to new problems and issues which emerge in society. Traditions which ossify and fail to accommodate social change die. Traditions of thought cannot only evolve and change but they contain features which endure over time. It is the basic unchanging structure of ideas which underpin a tradition of thought which we need to grasp in working out the implications of that tradition for our response to a particular historically situated social situation.

Education as a Social Practice

Perhaps the most trenchant analysis of the condition of contemporary Western society to be published in recent years was provided by Alasdair MacIntyre in *After Virtue*.[9] In this book MacIntyre argues that the condition is grave, and can only be redeemed if we protect and preserve forms of social life which conform to the Aristotelian ethical tradition. In chapter 14 MacIntyre sketches what he believes to be the core features of that tradition which I shall now attempt to summarise.

Central to the Aristotelian ethical tradition is the exercise of the virtues. The idea of virtue derives its sense from and can only be sustained in, social practices.

According to MacIntyre a social practice is:

> ... any coherent and complex form of socially established co-operative human activity through which goods internal to that form of activity are realised in the course of trying to achieve those standards of excellence which are appropriate to, and partially definitive of that form of activity, with the result that human powers to achieve excellence, and human conceptions of the ends and goods involved, are systematically extended.

MacIntyre argues that on this account of a social practice only some activities are complex enough to count as social practices. What are ruled out are activities which require a limited range of technical skills, e.g. throwing a football, bricklaying, planting turnips. However, these simple activities form part of more complex activities: playing football, architecture, farming. It is the latter which constitute social practices.

Social practices cannot be understood as aggregations of simple technical skill domains. Achieving excellence in a social practice is not just a matter of improving specific technical skills. It also involves having regard for the ends and values which define the practice, and developing those powers which are necessary if they are to be realised.

The distinction between goods (values) internal to a practice and goods external to it is a crucial one. External goods are only contingently connected to a practice. If one cannot obtain such things as prestige, status, or wealth as a result of participation in a certain practice there are always alternative means of obtaining them available. However, goods internal to a practice can only be obtained by engaging in that particular practice. They consist of complex abilities and skills which can only be developed in the pursuit of goals which are intrinsic to the practice and give it its point. This pursuit of intrinsic goals is governed by standards and principles of procedure against which performance in the activity is judged. MacIntyre claims that over time, conceptions of the goals intrinsic to a practice change, and with them the standards and principles which govern their pursuit. These in turn call forth new extensions of human powers and therefore new conceptions of the internal goods which can be achieved. By way of illustration MacIntyre shows how the goals of portrait painting have shifted from the iconic representations of Christ and the Saints, through the naturalist representations of actual faces in fifteenth-century Flemish and German painting, to the synthesis of Rembrandt where the naturalistic portrait of a particular individual is rendered in a novel iconic form.

It is in relation to Aristotelian accounts of a social practice that MacIntyre defines a virtue as:

.. an acquired human quality the possession and exercise of which tends to enable us to achieve those goods which are internal to practices and lack of which effectively prevents us from achieving any such goods.

In addition to virtues specific to a particular social practice, MacIntyre suggests there are certain virtues which are necessary to sustain social practices in general, e.g. those of justice, courage, and honesty. He also argues that any adequate concept of these more general virtues assumes some holistic view of the goals and goods of human life generally. Without such a view human life lacks unity and is pervaded with conflicts between incompatible social practices, e.g. between commitments to excellence in the arts and the claims of family life. One needs, he argues, some over-arching view of the purpose of life to be able to prioritise and organise our commitment to specific social practices.

MacIntyre uses his Aristotelian account of a social practice to throw light on the issue of competition versus co-operation in human activities. There is an important difference between external and internal goods. When the former are achieved they belong only to the individuals who achieve them. Those who fail to achieve them do not possess them. The achievement of external goods, given that not all can succeed, necessarily involves competition between individuals. However, those who achieve internal goods benefit the community of practitioners as a whole.

MacIntyre argues that when Turner 'transformed the seascape in painting' in a quite new way he 'enriched the whole relevant community'. Of course, MacIntyre points out, people do compete to excel in a social practice but their shared commitment to its goals enables them to appreciate and rejoice in the excellence achieved by others. While external goods only benefit individuals, internal goods benefit communities. They are common rather than individual goods. But even the excellence achieved by individuals within a social practice is the outcome of social co-operation operating though the exercise of virtues like treating others justly, being honest or truthful (not cheating), and putting oneself at risk to protect others from harm (moral courage). MacIntyre argues that:

> Without the virtues there could be a recognition only of what I have called external goods and not at all of internal goods in the context of practices. And in any society which recognised only external goods competitiveness would be the dominant and even exclusive feature.

Finally, MacIntyre is careful to distinguish a social practice from its institutional context. Institutions are necesary to sustain social practices. Medicine needs hospitals, education needs schools, and intellectual disciplines need universities. It is through an institution that people are initiated into a social practice, thereby learning to acquire its virtues and submitting themselves to its standards. However, institutions as such are inevitably concerned with the acquisition and distribution of external goods such as wealth, power and status. And indeed, MacIntyre argues, such concerns are necessary if institutions are to support and sustain social practices. The relationship between external and internal goods is an intimate one. But it does make social practices particularly vulnerable to the competitiveness of institutions. This is why the virtues are so important. 'Without justice, courage, and honesty', MacIntyre argues, 'practices could not resist the corrupting power of institutions.' In other words, the achievement of the virtues gives participants in a social practice the power not only to achieve excellence in their performance but to resist the corrupting influence of naked competition for wealth, status, and power.

Stenhouse on 'Education'

It is interesting to compare MacIntyre's reiteration of the Aristotelian tradition with Stenhouse's[10] discussion of the way in which the universal application of 'the objectives model' to curriculum planning would distort the nature of education. Stenhouse argues that education is necessarily comprised of four processes: training, instruction, initiation and induction. Training is concerned with the acquisition of skills involved in the performance of a specific task, e.g. making a canoe, learning a foreign language, typing, baking a cake, handling laboratory apparatus. His examples resemble Aristotle's *making* activities, and those proffered by MacIntyre as technical skill domains. Instruction is concerned with the acquisition and retention of information, e.g. tables of chemical elements, dates in history, the names of European countries, German irregular verbs, a pastry recipe. According to Stenhouse 'the objectives model' is appropriate to designing training and instructional processes. But although a necessary part of educational activity, these processes are not sufficient to make it educational.

Initiation is concerned with securing commitment and conformity to certain social norms and values. These are frequently not made explicit but are tacitly transmitted through the 'hidden curriculum'. Induction is concerned with giving access to knowledge. But knowledge is not the same as information. Rather, according to Stenhouse, it consititutes structures or systems of thinking, about ourselves and the world, which are encapsulated within our culture. For Stenhouse induction into systems of thought is central to any *educational* process. As features of such a process, training, instruction, and initiation are all subordinate processes. Moreover, Stenhouse argues, induction cannot be matched to 'the objectives model'. This is because knowledge is not information but structures 'to sustain creative thought and provide frameworks for judgement'. However, such structures are intrinsically problematic and contestable in the sense that the theories, concepts, and principles of which they consist are open to a variety of interpretations. Stenhouse argued, for example, that disputes among historians about the causes of war are not so much based on the evidence available to each party as on conflicting interpretations of the concept of historical causality. To translate 'structures' into 'objectives' or 'targets' is to distort the nature of knowledge.

Educationally speaking it is not sufficient to transmit inert information about ideas, concepts and theories to students in the form of definitions. In the process of induction the teacher represents them as critical standards (s)he brings to bear on students' thinking about problems in the subject matter. They are embedded in the questions (s)he poses, the evidence (s)he draws attention to, and the tests (s)he asks students to submit their thinking to. Moreover, the teacher should induct students in a manner which gives them access to the problematic and contestable nature of structures of knowledge. An educationally worthwhile process involves a reflexive attitude towards the nature of knowledge, on the part of both teacher and students. Dialogue between teacher and students, and discussion among students are procedural principles governing any educationally worthwhile induction into knowledge.

The process of induction is more concerned with the manner in which students think than with the precise outcome of that thinking. Inducting students into the structures of knowledge is not a matter of producing a standardised outcome, but of enabling them to think in the light of standards which define disciplined ways of thinking. The production of a uniformity of outcomes is an indication that students are not developing their own powers of understanding but merely reproducing the understandings of their teachers. Stenhouse writes:

> Consider the marking of history essays. The examination marker has a large number which he must monitor.
>
> As he reads them he often becomes aware that there is a depressing similarity about them. This is because the majority of teachers have been working to a behavioural objective ... From the piles of essays a few leap out at the marker as original, surprising, showing evidence of individual thinking. These, the unpredictable, are the successes.

He argues that:

> Education as induction into knowledge is successful to the extent that it makes the behavioural outcomes of the students unpredictable.

This account of the process of education makes it sound very much like a social practice. Knowledge as the end-in-view is not a product of an educational process which can be defined independently of it. It is the forms or systems of thought which shape the interaction between teachers and students and among students within an educational process. It refers to those standards of excellence which are brought to bear on students' thinking in a manner which activates and extends their natural powers of understanding. It is the development of these powers which constitutes the goods internal to education and the achievement of excellence within it. Ray Elliott has argued that the natural powers of the human understanding are exercised:

> in retention and anticipation: synthesis and synopsis: in the reduction of wholes to parts: in bracketing properties and aspects: in discovering the objects of feelings and impressions: in guesswork: in pushing ideas to their limits: in shifts of perspective of many kinds: in weighing pros and cons and sensing the balance: and so on.[11]

Knowledge constitutes the structures which have historically evolved in our society for performing these mental activities. Such structures are a medium in which to think and develop the powers of the understanding: powers which constitute internal qualities, rather than external products, of the mental activities Elliott cites.

One can think of the virtues which are necessary if people are to develop their powers of understanding within the educational process, e.g. those of curiosity, patience, tenacity, persistence, open-mindedness, intellectual courage, honesty with oneself, and humility.

According to Stenhouse it is only when we have clarified knowledge as a medium rather than a product of thinking that we are in a position to grasp the functions of norms, information, and skills within the educational process. We cannot break knowledge down into specific informational, skill, and normative components, and then treat them as objectives of an educational process. This kind of outlook will be familiar to all those teachers who have been advised to classify their curriculum aims as either 'concepts', 'skills', or 'attitudes'. To do this is to lose sight of the educative context in which information, skills, and attitudes need to be transmitted. For Stenhouse, education involves those other processes of transmission but it cannot be reduced to them without loss. They must always be subordinated to the overall aim of inducting students into structures of knowledge. In this context 'the objectives model' can be applied to designing instruction and training, but it always plays a subordinate role to 'the process model'.

Excellence, Standards and the Education Reform Act

In this section I shall critique, in the light of the previous section, the assumptions about excellence and standards embodied in the Bill which preceded the Education Reform Act. As a springboard I want to describe an episode which occurred during a delegation, which I attended, to the Secretary of State from the North of England conference in March of this year. In what appeared an unguarded moment Mr Baker, the Secretary of State for Education, confessed a concern that his Bill would do little to cater for creative learning. He experienced a tension between a curriculum which raised standards generally and one which catered for creativity. We all agreed that his curriculum left little space for creativity in learning, but did not have time on a crowded agenda to explore the issue further. So let me try now: it is unlikely that Mr Baker will read this paper, and even if he does it is rather too late for him to initiate the radical amendments to his Bill my argument will entail.

Mr Baker's problem, in all his talk about 'raising standards' and achieving 'excellence' in education, is that he has misunderstood the nature of educational standards and confused them with product specifications or 'standardisation'. This is because he has become trapped in a view of education as a manufacturing process or technology. In this context standards are concerned with securing a uniformity of product and defining fixed objectives or 'targets' as the government calls them: a military metaphor employed by business and industry as an orientation for the rational management of resources.

The Education Reform Act assumes that in setting targets the curriculum task groups will be establishing *educational* standards. Contrast this with Stenhouse's view that the quality of educational achievements is manifested in unpredictable and diverse performances. Induction into structures of knowledge does not standardise students' thinking but supports creativity and originality of thought. Mr Baker's 'dilemma' is experienced as such because he assumes that 'standards' define ends external to educational processes. If he viewed them as structures of thought which support the development of those natural powers which constitute goods internal to education and which manifest themselves in unpredictable and diverse performances, then he would experience no dilemma between 'raising standards' and an education for creativity.

The logic of 'technical rationality' pervades the Education Reform Act. Task groups are busy analysing the subjects specified in the national curriculum into testable attainment targets. The government assumes that that does not involve any consideration of programmes of study and processes. This will come later as the responsibility of the new National Curriculum Council. However much the members of those groups attempt to incorporate an educational perspective into the target-setting enterprise, the logic of 'technical rationality' will defeat them in the end. Once educational standards are specified as measurable targets, which can be defined independently of the content and process of education, teachers have little option but to distort the practice of education and the role standards play in it. Stenhouse neatly illustrates the consequences of target setting when he argues:

> Literary skills are to be justified as helping us to read Hamlet. Hamlet must not be justified as a training ground for literary skills.[12]

It is difficult to see how, under the provisions of the Act, teachers will be able to justify the content of education other than in terms of its instrumentality for achieving extrinsically related targets. A good example of the gradual capitulation of the task groups to the ruthless logic of 'technical rationality' can be found in the saga of the Maths group. The original task group broke up in disarray after the majority refused to identify specific attainment targets for ages 7, 11, 14 and 16 and reaffirmed the emphasis in modern maths on the development of understanding. Professor Sig Prais resigned. He evidently believed that an emphasis on computational skills was the only way we could match the performance of German, French and Japanese students. He is a member of the National Institute of Economic and Social Research, which spends a great deal of time undertaking cross-national comparative studies of achievement.

The task group reconvened under Duncan Graham, the ex-Chief Education Officer for Suffolk and the (then) Chairman of the National Curriculum Council. The group produced attainment targets. According to the *Observer* (14 August 1988) the report reflects a continuing tendency to make computational skill subordinate to 'understanding'. Although structures of knowledge are represented as targets according to the rhetoric of government, they can easily be reinterpreted by teachers as criteria governing the process of learning. But Mr Baker is no fool. He is reported as intending to overrule the advice that long divisions and multiplications need not be done without calculators, and he 'will also make clear his concern that practical and applied maths should be closely related to facts and skills'. Evidently some members of the group wanted mathematical understanding assessed on the basis of its application to practical problems, while others, supported by the Prime Minister, wanted pencil and paper tests.

The whole saga appears to revolve around whether information about mathematical facts and computational skills should primarily constitute the standards of maths teaching or whether pupils should be inducted into the structures of mathematical reasoning about practical maths problems. From the report in the *Observer* it seems that Mr Baker is intent on ensuring that teachers treat mathematical problems as instrumental to the acquisition of facts and technical skills. In so doing it will be extremely difficult for teachers to induct pupils into the structures of mathematical knowledge in a manner which will develop their powers of understanding. What is at stake here is the very idea of mathematical education as a social practice and the achievement of excellence in relation to those goods which are internal to the process of developing mathematical understanding.

At another level one can argue that this saga of political manipulation has little to do with *educational* standards and excellence as such. Firstly, it is about designing a competitive system of schooling: one which enables achievements to be compared with other advanced industrial countries. The only way this can be done is to specify achievements as quantifiable outcomes. And one can only do this if they are posited as goods which are extrinsic to the educational process; as information and skills which render those individuals who possess them saleable commodities on the labour market. The theory is that if we gear schooling towards the acquisition of marketable facts and skills our school system will not only compete successfully with other industrial societies, but this success will enable us to achieve supremacy in the industrial enterprise of wealth creation.

Within an enterprise which is exclusively concerned with transforming human beings into marketable commodities there is little room for pupils to achieve those goods which are internal to educational practices — goods which can only be described as excellences of 'being'. The problem with the Education Reform Act is that it divorces 'standards' from 'human excellence'. And this is why there is no room for creativity. An educational system which exclusively aims to transform people into commodities for consumption on the labour market must treat them in turn as passive consumers. The curriculum will consist of objects to be possessed in the form of facts and skills rather than of objects of thought-situations, problems and issues which are capable of challenging, activating, and extending natural powers of being. Only a curriculum of the latter kind can provide a context for the achievement of human excellence.

To borrow Erich Fromm's distinction between the 'being' and 'having' modes of human existence, I would argue that the Education Reform Act constitutes a comprehensive plan for generating an 'education for having' and eliminating any 'subversive' attempts to establish an 'education for being'.[13] It reinforces a view of pupils and their parents as possessive individuals or consumers. For pupils the race is on for the prizes of possessing more information and skills than others. The target specifications provide the scale against which individual rates of consumption can be compared.

Parents are not viewed as active participants in an educational process collaborating with teachers to enable their children to develop their natural powers of understanding. Instead they are viewed as passive beneficiaries of the products of education. Much is made of their freedom to choose an education for their children. But it is the freedom of the consumer to buy the product he or she desires and not the freedom of parents to nurture the personal growth of their children.

The dominant theme running through the Education Reform Act is that of competitiveness. It is promoted at every level of education: between pupils, their parents, their teachers, and the schools. This theme not only underpins the national curriculum proposals, but also the infrastructures established by the Act: the opting out clause, open-enrolment, teacher appraisal, the new powers and responsibilities of school governors. Every aspect of the Act plays its part in promoting competition rather than collaboration. A key feature of the general strategy has been to recognise only those outcomes and goods which can be considered as external to the process of education. In this way education is transformed into a consumer-orientated production process whose effectiveness is promoted by competition within both the consumer and delivery systems.

Consistent with this strategy has been the determination of the government to resist and bypass professional educationalists: teachers and their unions, LEA officials and advisers/inspectors, Her Majesty's Inspectorate, educational researchers and teacher trainers. As we have seen with the Maths and Science task groups, there has been a tendency for 'the professionals' in them to try to safeguard ends, values, and standards which are internal to educational practices. The intention to restrict the influence of educationalists is surely the point of the clause which requires teachers to seek the permission of the Secretary of State before they attempt any innovations which may not fit the framework established in the Act.

The threat any recognition of internal goods and standards poses for the government is that they imply a commitment to collaborative activities at all levels of education. Pupils develop their powers of understanding, not in social isolation from their peers, but through discussion and the sharing of ideas about problems and issues. Discussion lies at the heart of an educative process. The achievement of individual excellence within this process depends upon the social co-operation of others in establishing the conditions of worthwhile discussion. Moreover, it benefits all the pupils in the class because it enhances their capacities to understand the problem addressed. Competition between individuals to excel in an educational process is contained within a shared recognition that the development of an individual's powers of understanding is a common good because it benefits the whole group.

In failing to recognise the internal values of education the Education Reform Act leaves little space for the development of those virtues which characterise the structure of social co-operation within any educative discourse. The Act divorces not only 'standards' from the achievement of 'excellence' in education, but also those virtues which are necessary conditions of such achievement. They constitute the forms of social co-operation implicit in the educative process. Such forms can be sustained in classrooms only if they permeate the ethos of the institutions in which they are situated — namely, schools. These institutions have had to balance supporting an educative process against distributing extrinsic goods among pupils, e.g. the possession of marketable 'knowledge' and skills. The Education Reform Act threatens that balance by sanctioning competitiveness as the dominant and prevailing ethos within and between schools.

It is sheer hypocrisy on the government's part to claim, as it does within the text of the Act, that the national curriculum is concerned with the intellectual, moral, and spiritual development of pupils in schools. The logic of technical rationality which permeates it is quite inconsistent with all these aims. It leaves little space for personal development in either its intellectual, moral, or spiritual aspects, as I shall now attempt to demonstrate.

Academic Achievement and Personal Development

In my earlier account of MacIntyre's analysis of a social practice, I referred to the importance he attributes to locating social practices in some unified vision of the purpose of human life. The account Stenhouse gave of the educational process as induction into knowledge needs to be extended at this point. Education is not simply a matter of developing human powers of understanding by inducting students into 'structures of knowledge'. It is about developing these powers in relation to the things which matter in life. Chess is a sophisticated and complex activity which provides opportunities for people to develop a range of complex skills and abilities. But it is nevertheless a game. The problems of chess have little significance as problems of living. It is in relation to the latter that the powers of human understanding must be developed if such a process is to count as an educational one.

Problems of living are not technical problems of discovering the means for achieving ends which can be clearly specified in advance of the solution. They constitute problems about how the various possibilities for action in a situation relate to the overriding purpose of living. Their solution is not a matter of clarifying the purpose of living and then choosing a course which will achieve it. It is a matter of locating a course of action which is coherent with a unified conception of living. Problems of living arise when situations do not obviously yield courses of action which fit a unified conception of purpose in life. Such problems challenge our prior conceptions of purpose. Any resolution must not only consist of the discovery of an appropriate course of action but also a more developed conception of the purpose of life.

Spiritual development proceeds by resolving problems of living wisely. Wisdom can be defined as the achievement of a sense of unity of purpose in the multiplicity of decisions and acts which constitute a human life. Education is a process which not only inducts into structures of knowledge, but brings those structures into play with the problems of living, thereby utilising them in the service of wisdom.

The process I have described as spiritual development is an aspect of personal development. It constitutes the primary end of the educational process as a whole. Its realisation should not be confined to a slot on the school curriculum called 'Religious Education' or 'Personal and Social Education'. The existence of such slots exemplifies the displacement of the aims of the whole curriculum to part of that whole. It is evidence of the way in which 'structures of knowledge' have been detached from their educative function of developing our powers to handle the problems of living wisely.

Maxwell argues that:

If 'religion' is characterised in a broad way as 'concern for what is of most value in human existence' then academic inquiry . . . is essentially a religious enterprise.[14]

His argument draws on a contrast between two views of intellectual inquiry. Central to one view, that of 'the philosophy of knowledge', is the doctrine that intellectual inquiry must be totally detached from and uninfluenced by, the investigator's practical concerns and interests. Central to the other view, that of 'the philosophy of wisdom', is the doctrine that:

The intellectual progress and success of academic inquiry is to be judged in terms of the extent to which academic work produces and makes available ideas, proposals, arguments, discoveries, techniques that help people achieve what is of value in life in a co-operative and just way.

These two different doctrines, according to Maxwell, have radically different implications for education. Intellectual inquiry shaped by 'the philosophy of knowledge' posits two quite separate types of learning: 'On the one hand there is academic learning; on the other hand there is learning how to live.' However, if intellectual inquiry is shaped by the 'philosophy of wisdom', the dichotomy disappears: 'Academic learning *is* learning about how to live.'

If we construe education as a process of induction into knowledge that is related to the things which matter for living then its intrinsic goods can be classified according to three of its interrelated dimensions of personal development: the intellectual, moral, and spiritual. The intellectual goods consist of the development of the powers of human understanding in relation to the problems of living. The spiritual goods consist of the development of wisdom through the exercise of these intellectual powers, and the moral goods consist of those virtues or attitudes which are necessary conditions for developing the powers of the understanding and discovering solutions to the fundamental problems of living.

In spite of its espoused aims of promoting the intellectual, moral, and spiritual development of pupils, the government's national curriculum detaches academic learning from 'learning how to live' and at best caters for the latter in lower status slots in the curriculum. Separating 'academic learning' from 'learning about how to live' makes it easier to construe knowledge as information and skills rather than as dynamic structures within which to think about the problems of living. It also makes the achievements of learning easier and less costly 'things' to test and compare.

The task group for Science appears to have struggled hard to accommodate the idea of targets to their conception of a worthwhile scientific education. They have consistently argued that induction into science should not be detached from the study of practical problems of living which raise questions about fundamental human values. The Maths group appears to have wanted to adopt a similar line although they have not to my knowledge been so explicit about the sorts of practical problems they have in mind — whether their concern is with the application of maths to technical problems or with its application to more fundamental problems in real life.

In the *Independent* (17 August, 1988) Simon Midgely reported that Mr Baker 'has serious reservations about the weight both groups attribute to the importance of children applying scientific and mathematical knowledge in the real world'. Evidently Mr Baker 'feels that more emphasis still needs to be placed on basic knowledge and understanding in each subject'. It would not be too presumptuous to interpret the demand for more emphasis on 'basic knowledge and understanding' as a demand for more emphasis on specific items of information and facts. As I suggested previously, the pressure is towards abstracting and isolating information and skills from their appropriate location in an educative process. What Mr Baker and the government fail to realise is that the emphasis they want actually undermines planning a curriculum which is capable of fostering personal development in each of the dimensions cited as aims in the Act: namely, the intellectual, moral, and spiritual.

In his article Midgely refers to the government's concern to lift the performance of average and below average children, 'the bottom 40 per cent'. The concern is shared by the task groups. However, there may be in operation two different diagnoses of the problem. The government appears to assume that these pupils lack 'basic' information and skills because they have not been taught them systematically. The idea of specifying them as targets is a device for ensuring that they will be in future. The alternative diagnosis, which may well find subscribers in the task groups, is that the 'basics' have not been learned. And this is not necessarily because they were not taught, but because pupils were not required to learn them in a context which activated and challenged their intellectual powers in relation to the things that really matter in life. In other words, such learning made little sense because these pupils could not fit it into any meaningful context of living. Perhaps they were less willing than their more 'achieving' peers to spend time and effort learning meaningless information and skills. If the second diagnosis is correct then the specification of attainment targets will do little for the bottom 40 per cent. What is required is a national plan which starts not with target specifications but with a map of the dimensions of human experience which matter for contemporary living. The next step would be to select content which exemplifies problems, dilemmas, and issues of living which experience confronts in these dimensions. *Hamlet*'s educational value lies not primarily in its instrumentality for learning literacy skills, but in the fact that it speaks to the human condition.

Such a curriculum map of the content of education would specify not information to be learned but situations to be addressed. It is only when this kind of map has been developed that we are in a position to select knowledge structures which might enable pupils to develop their understanding of 'life situations' and to select those specific items of information and technical skills which need to be acquired in the process of such development.

Stenhouse argued that from the standpoint of the 'process model' the starting point for curriculum design was the mapping of content rather than of objectives. From this point of view the procedures embedded in the development of the national curriculum are bound to treat content as of instrumental value. Rather than set up task groups to define targets prior to the specification of the programmes of study by the new Curriculum Council, a 'process model' approach would have begun with a map of the kinds of situations to be addressed in developing powers of understanding, and in acquiring relevant information and skills. And there is no reason why parents, employers and members of the public generally could not be involved in developing such a map. It is a task for society as a whole. The task of the professional educators is a different one, which I shall now turn to.

Earlier I suggested that Stenhouse's 'process model' made explicit in a coherent form many of the ideas already implicit in the curriculum reform practices of teachers during the 1960s in innovatory secondary modern schools. These teachers were also trying to resolve the problem of underachieving pupils. In a previous paper I have claimed that their practices embodied a curriculum theory which consisted of a cluster of interrelated ideas about education, learning, curriculum, and teaching.[15] The key elements of this theory were as follows:

(1) Education is a process in which pupils develop their intellectual powers by utilising public structures of knowledge in constructing personal understandings of life situations. Within an educational process, differing understandings of the same situation may manifest similar intellectual powers. It is only when knowledge is exclusively regarded as information to be reproduced through memory learning that understanding is presumed to consist of a uniform learning outcome.

(2) Learning involves the active construction rather than the passive reproduction of meaning.

(3) Learning is assessed in terms of the development of intellectual powers manifested in its outcomes, rather than in terms of the match between pre-determined performance standards and behavioural outcomes. The educational quality of the latter can be described and judged but not standardised as performance indicators and measured.

(4) Teaching aims to enable or facilitate the development of pupils' natural powers of understanding (rather than to produce certain pre-determined behavioural outcomes). It is concerned with establishing enabling conditions.

(5) The criteria for evaluating teaching differ from those for evaluating learning. In evaluating teaching the criteria employed refer to conditions which enable pupils to develop their powers. But these are not causal conditions. They establish opportunities for pupils to develop their powers of understanding. Whether pupils take these opportunities is another matter.

In evaluating learning the criteria employed should refer to qualities of mind actually manifested in the performance of pupils. What counts as useful curriculum knowledge cannot be determined in advance of the pedagogical process. It is determined on the basis of teachers' own reflective deliberations as they select and organise theories, concepts, and ideas in response to pupils' search for personal meaning. 'Structures of knowledge', information, and skills can only be pre-selected as resources for learning. The appropriateness of these resources for developing pupils' powers in relation to life situations can only be tested in a pedagogical process of teacher-based action-research. Curriculum development and teaching are not two distinct processes. The former is a dimension of the latter.

This curriculum theory, embedded in curriculum reform practices initiated by teachers, is consistent with the theory of education I have expounded in this paper. It also explains the emphasis Stenhouse placed on the development of teachers as curriculum researchers, and his slogan that 'there can be no curriculum development without teacher development'.

The theory enables us to develop further an alternative approach to the development of the national curriculum. I have already suggested that a 'process model' would begin with a societal mapping of the kinds of life situations pupils need to address in developing their powers of understanding. The next stage, for the National Curriculum Council, would be to review all areas of knowledge in the light of the problems, dilemmas and issues framework. This would not only entail revisions to the content of established curriculum subjects but the introduction of quite new subject areas, e.g. medicine, law, or architecture. We might end up with a rather different set of subject areas from those proposed in the Education Reform Act.

The next questions would be: How do we know that the selections of knowledge are useful? And: What is the best way of organising this knowledge for pedagogical purposes? These questions can only be answered on the basis of teacher experiment and reflection in classrooms. Moreover, it is unlikely that one would be able to secure agreement about what counts as useful knowldedge and how it is best organised for pedagogical purposes. This is because so much will depend on the different classroom and school contexts in which teachers operate. What constitutes useful knowledge in one context may prove useless in another. And what constitutes a pedagogically supportive form of curriculum organisation in one context may undermine the quality of the pedagogy in another.

Within 'the process model' there are limits to what can be nationally specified. What is important is the concept of the national curriculum as a resource to support reflective pedagogical practice in schools, and the establishment of mechanisms by which central government can continuously modify its curriculum map in the light of feedback from teachers and schools.

The whole enterprise ultimately rests on the quality of teachers. The kind of curriculum development process I have outlined certainly assumes a teaching profession capable of improving the quality of education through reflective pedagogical practice. But then, in my view, there is no alternative way of improving education. The alternative proposed in the Education Reform Act is to abandon the concept of an educational practice and to transform schooling into a production process in which teachers are deprofessionalised into technical operatives administering prescribed treatments in the light of the prescribed product specifications. The idea of teachers as professionals only makes sense within a context in which education is viewed as a social practice.

Notes and references

This paper was the Lawrence Stenhouse Memorial Lecture delivered at the fourteenth annual conference of the British Educational Research Association, University of Easst Anglia, 1–3 September 1988.
 1. Kerr, J (1968) The problem of curriculum reform. In J. Kerr (ed.) *Changing the Curriculum.* London: University of London Press.
 2. Stenhouse, L.A, (1975) *An Introduction to Curriculum Research and Development.* London: Heinemann. Chapters 6 and 7.
 3. Peters, R.S. (1959) *Authority, Responsibility and Education.* London: Allen & Unwin.
 4. Elliott, J. (1988) Teachers as researchers: Implications for supervision and teacher education. Address given at the AERA annual conference, New Orleans.
 5. Stenhouse, L.A. (1968) The Humanities Curriculum Project. *Journal of Curriculum Studies* 23, 1.
 6. Stenhouse, L.A. (1971) The Humanities Curriculum Project: The rationale. *Theory into Practice* 10, 154–62.
 7. Elliott, J. (1983) Self-evaluation: Professional development and accountability. In M. Galton and R. Moon (eds) *Changing Schools . . . Changing Curriculum* (ch. 15). London: Harper & Row.
 8. Gadamer, H.G. (1975) *Truth and Method.* New York: Seabury Press.
 9. MacIntyre, A. (1983) *After Virtue: A Study in Moral Theory* (2nd edn). London: Duckworth.
10. Stenhouse, L.A. (1975) op. cit.
11. Elliott, R.K. (1975) Education and human behaviour. In S.C. Brown (ed.) *Philosophers Discuss Education.* London: Macmillan.
12. Stenhouse, L.A. (1975) op. cit.
13. Fromm, E. (1976) *To Have or to Be?* Published in the ABACUS edition by Sphere Books, 1979.
14. Maxwell, N. (1984) *From Knowledge to Wisdom.* Oxford: Basil Blackwell. Chapter 4.
15. Elliott, J. (1988) op. cit.

5 Some Ambiguities in Stenhouse's Notion of 'The Teacher as Researcher': Towards a New Resolution

STEPHEN KEMMIS

Substantial changes have taken place in social theory and education studies since Lawrence Stenhouse's death in 1982. The resources of social theory that have by now become commonplace appeared then to be the arcane concerns of a few specialists: in the English-speaking world at least, the work of Michel Foucault was still more or less unknown in education studies; even Hans-Georg Gadamer, Jurgen Habermas and Anthony Giddens were still securing their places in the pantheon of *educational* research methodology. In education studies at that time, Michael Apple and Paul Willis had begun to establish themselves as an *avant-garde*; Henry Giroux and Dale Spender were still rising stars.

Reaching still further back to 1975, when Stenhouse's *An Introduction to Curriculum Research and Development* appeared, the new ground was being broken in education by such researchers as Basil Bernstein, David Hamilton and Michael F.D. Young in Britain, and elsewhere by such people as Samuel Bowles and Herbert Gintis, Bob Connell, Lee Cronbach, Daniel Kallós and Ulf Lundgren, Bob Stake and Lou Smith. In 1975, there were still some new points to be made in the debate over behavioural objectives, and the debates over methodology in educational research and evaluation were still invigorating. Though the throne of empiricism in educational research was still at the water's edge, the theoretical tide had turned and it was rising. And at that time, under Stenhouse's leadership, the Centre for Applied Research in Education at the University of East Anglia was in its fifth year, becoming widely known as a hothouse for new ideas, variously regarded as controversial, eccentric, heretical, maverick, visionary, and original.

Although risking the banality of pointing out that Lawrence Stenhouse was a man of his time, I want to argue that he was on the brink of major changes in educational theory and research: that he was, in an important sense, a *transitional* figure, though his work was of far more than transitory interest. To use Kuhn's[1] distinction, Stenhouse was interested in finding opportunities to do 'extraordinary' things against the necessary background of 'ordinary' educational research going on around him.

For example, Stenhouse brought a unique and original perspective to bear on the abiding problem of theory and practice in education, and he changed the character of the problem: he recognised that large-scale curriculum research and development did not necessarily bring improvements in local educational practice, and that it would always require teacher research — local research by teachers into their own particular practices — to achieve lasting improvements in the quality of education. Since Stenhouse, it is no longer possible to think about improving schools or curricula simply as a matter of changing the resources available to teachers, or even in terms of changing what teachers do (as if what teachers do were the property of educational administrators, or boards of governors, or secretaries of state for education). Now we know that sustainable improvements in education cannot normally be achieved without teachers' commitment to the intellectual and scientific task of researching their own practice, as a part of the wider process of improving the curriculum, the school, and the work of education for communities and whole societies.

So, even if Stenhouse was a prisoner of his intellectual history and his times, it seems to me that he made more than his share of trips over the wall. Nevertheless, he remained bound into uncertainties and ambiguities which it is now possible to see somewhat more clearly — for example, in relation to questions such as that of the relationship between theory and practice in education.

In claiming that new developments were possible partly because Stenhouse was opening a new frontier for educational research, one is immediately reminded of Michael Scriven's warning that

> intellectual progress is possible only because newcomers can stand on the shoulders of giants. This feat is often confused with treading on their toes, particularly but not only by the newcomer.[2]

In the first Lawrence Stenhouse Memorial Lecture in 1988, John Elliott discussed aspects of Stenhouse's views of curriculum and ventured a response to the radical Educational Reform Act introduced by the (then) Secretary of State for Education, Kenneth Baker. Curriculum development is one of two 'main thrusts' of Stenhouse's work identified in a paper by Jean Rudduck.[3] In this lecture, I will address myself to some questions concerning the second of these 'thrusts': Stenhouse's views of educational research and, in particular, teacher research.

Lawrence Stenhouse and Educational Research

I propose to focus on Stenhouse's views of educational research primarily as outlined in *An Introduction to Curriculum Research and Development*,[4] from which follows a continuous line of writing about teacher research, some of which is picked up in *Authority, Education and Emancipation*.[5] I will refer only in passing to his writings on case study, case records and the contemporary history of education. This focus permits me to address what I take to be Stenhouse's most important contribution to educational research: his view of the teacher as researcher.[6]

Choosing this focus may suggest that I regard the vast array of his educational research and writing before 1975 as no more than a precursor to *An Introduction to Curriculum Research and Development*, and the work that follows it as no more than a denouement. Let me say at the outset that I do not.[7] His (1967) book, *Culture and Education*, still bears re-reading, though it has been overtaken by contemporary writings on curriculum and cultural reproduction and transformation which use more sophisticated analytical tools than were readily available in the late 1960s. Clearly, his directorship of the Humanities Curriculum Project (HCP) was of central importance not only to the development of his own thinking, but also to any account of curriculum and curriculum development in the 1960s and the 1970s.[8] To pick just a few highlights: through HCP, Stenhouse made a signal contribution to the teaching of the humanities, the development of the pedagogy of 'neutral chairmanship', and (after the project drew to a formal close) in collaboration with colleagues, to teaching in the area of race relations[9] and to the pedagogy of small group discussion.[10] As Jean Rudduck[11] has pointed out, his writings reveal a remarkable continuity of concern with the theme of authority and emancipation in education.

In *An Introduction to Curriculum Research and Development*, his earlier ideas about the emancipation of students through education are complemented by his development of the theme of emancipation of teachers through teacher research. His primary, 'positive' line of attack here was to propose an alternative view of educational research in which teachers had a central role to play in educational research; this was supplemented by a second line of attack aimed at demonstrating the frailties of conventional educational research and development. This secondary line is developed in a variety of writings on HCP, and distilled in the assault on the objectives model of curriculum development and evaluation in *An Introduction to Curriculum Research and Development*. In subsequent years, he pursued with vigour both the 'positive' argument for teacher research[12] and the 'negative' argument against conventional modes of educational research. The 'negative' argument was concentrated, on the one hand, on experimental research in education (for example, in his exploration of the notion of generalisation)[13] and, on the other, on problems and issues in 'illuminative' and 'case study' research[14] — leading him to propose what Leo Bartlett and I described as a 'quasi-historical' approach to case study[15] and the use of case studies as a basis for 'contemporary history of education'.[16]

The main lines of the argument of *An Introduction to Curriculum Research and Development* are well known. After clearing the ground and building a definition of 'curriculum', Stenhouse presents the behavioural objectives approach to curriculum development and offers his critique. He has two major objections to the objectives model: (a) it takes a mistaken view of the nature of knowledge, and (b) it mistakes the nature of the process of improving educational practice. His alternative — the 'process' model of curriculum design and development combined with the notion of 'the teacher as researcher' — is intended to meet these objections. On the one hand, he shows how significant knowledge and understandings for students are developed through procedures which do not pre-specify learning outcomes, but rather invite critical enquiry which takes students outside the realms teachers or curriculum developers might specify as *their* goals for students. On the other hand, he shows how teachers, too, must reach their own knowledge and understandings through critical and creative enquiry. Only on the basis that teachers develop their own practice, he argues, can sustainable improvements in education be secured.

'[C]urriculum research and development ought to belong to the teacher', he argued, 'and . . . there are prospects for making this good in practice. I concede that it will take a generation of work, and if the majority of teachers — rather than only the enthusiastic few — are to possess this field of research . . . the teacher's professional self-image and conditions of work will have to change' (p. 142). Stenhouse develops the notion of 'the teacher as researcher' along lines suggested by Hoyle's[17] idea of 'extended professionalism'. In Stenhouse's words, its critical characteristics involved:

> The commitment to systematic questioning of one's own teaching as a basis for development;
>
> The commitment and the skills to study one's own teaching;
>
> The concern to question and to test theory in practice by the use of those skills. (p. 144)

And again:

> . . . the outstanding characteristic of the extended professional is a capacity for autonomous professional self-development through systematic self-study, through the study of the work of other teachers and through the testing of ideas by classroom research procedures. (p. 144)

After reviewing possible techniques of classroom study (Flanders' interaction analysis, content analysis of the logic of teaching, the 'social anthropological' approach, and the use of participant observers) and identifying some of their limitations, he examines theoretical and methodological problems confronting teachers wishing to undertake classroom research (generalisation, objectivity, and the like), concluding that there are great difficulties to be confronted, and that there is a need to evolve 'styles of co-operative research by teachers and using full-time researchers to support the teachers' work' (p. 162). Nevertheless, he believed that it was worth facing the tensions between the role of teacher and researcher for

> ... in the end it is difficult to see how teaching can be improved or how curricular proposals can be evaluated without self monitoring on the part of teachers. A research tradition which is accessible to teachers and which feeds teaching must be created if education is to be significantly improved. (p. 165)

Much has been written in support of the idea of 'teachers as researchers' – indeed, I have written some of it myself.[18] Much of the current literature is less circumspect about the prospects for teacher research than Stenhouse was in 1975, but that is perhaps because there is now such a large body of teachers and academic researchers committed to the practice of teacher research. In *An Introduction to Curriculum Research and Development*[19] and in *Authority, Emancipation and Education*,[20] Stenhouse particularly noted how the work of the Ford Teaching Project (conducted by John Elliott and Clem Adelman)[21] had demonstrated the power of the 'self-monitoring style of teaching' encouraged in HCP. It might reasonably be argued that the British and Australian 'rediscoveries' of action research were built on the foundation Stenhouse laid, quickly leading to the development of the action research 'movement'. But Stenhouse did not leave it to others to harvest the field he had sown; as the collection of papers edited by Rudduck & Hopkins[22] shows, long after *An Introduction to Curriculum Research and Development*, he continued to refine his ideas about teacher research and its relation to educational research by academic researchers.

Some Ambiguities in Stenhouse's View of Teacher Research

I will now draw attention to several ambiguities in Stenhouse's view of teacher research. My aim here is partly to show that he was, as I suggested earlier, a transitional figure, on the brink of important developments in social and educational research. But I also aim to show that these ambiguities reveal some of the limitations of his views of research, preventing him from resolving the very difficulties he wanted to resolve. From this, I believe, we may draw some conclusions about the conduct of contemporary educational research, for I hope to show that the problems with which Stenhouse struggled still need to be struggled over, and that we educational researchers still have a long way to go in our arguments about them.

These are the problems I wish to address:

(1) Ambiguities in Stenhouse's view of theory and its relation to practice.
(2) Ambiguities in his view of the relationship between theory and practice as an individual process and as a 'public' process (the equivocation between theory-and-practice, on the one hand, and knowledge-and-action, on the other).
(3) Ambiguities in his view of the relationship between academic theorists of education and classroom practitioners.
(4) Ambiguities in his views about the politics of change, especially in relation to social movements, the social order and the profession.

Having very briefly reviewed these ambiguities, I wish to argue that Stenhouse attempted to resolve these issues in ways which not only prevented him from reaching an adequate resolution, but actually maintained the very problems he sought to overcome. For example, by placing the stress he did on 'co-operative' relationships between academic theorists and classroom practitioners, it may be argued that he helped to entrench rather than to reconstruct the division of labour between researchers and teachers.

Others before and after Stenhouse have made progress in exploring the central issue of theory and practice in terms of the metatheories which underpin particular kinds of relations between theory and practice, theorising and practising, theorists and practitioners. But recourse to metatheoretical perspectives on educational research cannot, of itself, resolve the issues.[23] I want to argue that the issues of theory and practice that Stenhouse correctly identified as central to the improvement of education through educational research are not only metatheoretical issues but also practical ones — and practical issues of a certain kind which I will describe as *metapractical*. Addressed as metapractical questions, I will argue, they suggest new and more adequate resolutions. Thus I will conclude that it is not just a matter of changing the way we construe the problems of educational theory and practice in educational research if we are to resolve them; it is a question of changing the concrete, material practices through which we educational researchers relate to educational practitioners. Put bluntly, it means *not* doing our work the way we do it now; it means doing our work differently. Perhaps, in the final analysis, this means: doing different work.

Theory and its relation to practice

At the risk of placing too much burden on the very few words in Stenhouse's definition of curriculum, I want to use it as a point of departure for analysing his view of theory and its relationship to practice. He was critical of many standard definitions, so he fashioned his own:

A curriculum is an attempt to communicate the essential principles of an educational proposal in such a form that it is open to critical scrutiny and capable of effective translation into practice.[24]

It is a revealing definition. It emphasises that curriculum is problematic — as much a source of questions as it is an answer to them. So far so good. But then the problems begin.

A key word in the definition is the apparently innocuous 'translation': it suggests a fundamental categorical separation between the word and the world — that there is, on the one side, a linguistic realm inhabited by (among other things) 'principles' and, on the other, a world of mute though powerful action: 'practice'. In accepting the image of 'translation' Stenhouse is led into an *empiricist view of the relationship between theory and practice* — a separation between the world of concepts and the material world studied by science. Once accepting this view, he is led towards the orthodox but conceptually dangerous view that the abstracted and universalised practices referred to in most theories of education are the same practices as the concrete, material practices of particular teachers in particular classrooms. Clearly, Stenhouse struggled against this implication, repeatedly referring to the need for theorists to develop their theories close to the action in classrooms, and for practitioners to test theories for themselves to discover their practical utility.

The empiricist view of theory and practice suggests that the use of words in communication is not itself a form of action — communicative action. There is no easy break between the world of words, the world of action, and the (natural physical) world of things acted upon.[25] Once the notion of categorical separation — the gap — between principle and practice has been accepted, it requires 'bridging' ('translation').[26] Stenhouse argued that teachers and curriculum developers should constantly strive to do this bridging: mediating between principle and practice by acting on principle and by being critical about their work. But is this work of 'bridging' — this 'translating' — itself in the realm of principle or practice? Or is it done at another level of theory and practice (for example, the realm of metatheory or metapractice)? And, if it is at a meta-level, is there still another realm above this which determines how metaprinciples should be related to metapractices? And are there other realms beyond that?

In short, the dichotomy of principle and practice enshrined in the empiricist image of 'translation' seems to me to lead into a *reductio ad absurdum*. The issue can be resolved, however, by recourse to metatheoretical literature,[27] and especially those views of theory and practice which emphasise the reflexivity of their relationship.[28] Put another way, it may be argued that principle (or theory) and practice are mutually constitutive[29]: practices have at their heart an agreement among actors to orient themselves within a shared social framework and a shared framework of meaning in their action.[30] What makes a practice 'educational', for example, is a commitment to acting, with others, in ways which can be understood as educational because they refer to shared traditions of educational practice, and because they can be judged in relation to criteria furnished by those traditions.

Beyond the problem of empiricism, Stenouse's definition also implies *a rationalistic theory of action*[31] — the theory that actions are the realisations of meanings (including principles, aspirations or plans, for example). In suggesting that a curriculum is an 'attempt to communicate ... an educational proposal', the definition characterises curriculum as something conceived outside the field of practice; something prior to practice. In using the idea of a 'proposal', he aimed to distinguish his view from one set of definitions of curriculum which emphasised 'whatever happens in schools' — thus, in his view,[32] reducing the study of curriculum to the study of whatever goes on in schools. But he also wanted to distinguish curriculum from another set of definitions which see the curriculum 'as an intention, plan or prescription, an idea about what one would like to happen in schools.[33] His idea of the 'proposal', subject to critical scrutiny and to be tested in practice, was meant to avoid the instrumental, technical view of curriculum and curriculum research which would, in his view, follow from accepting an intentionalist definition. Rather than assuming that principles provided a guide for practice, or that pedagogical practice followed curriculum aspirations, he sought a formulation in which *both* principles and practice could be treated as problematic. Thus, in his view, 'the central problem of curriculum study is the gap between our ideas and aspirations and our attempts to operationalise them'.[34]

In his formulation, he had (in my view) correctly identified the problem of the relationship between theory and practice as central to a coherent account of education and educational research, but his resolution of the problem was, finally, unacceptable. He did not escape the snare he had identified. He correctly observed that a key difficulty of curriculum study was that it conceived of its role in terms of getting practice to conform to intentions or plans, but his notion of 'proposal', while problematising the plan, did not eliminate it as a key theoretical category. Even though Stenhouse was less subject to it than most of his contemporaries, his use of the idea of the 'proposal' in the end implied a rationalistic theory of action.[35] Despite his early misgivings about curriculum prespecification which threatened control of teachers,[36] despite his view that curriculum developers' proposals were only a source of ideas rather than an adequate description for the work of teachers, and despite this later image of curriculum as a medium in which teachers could improvise and explore and thus extend their art,[37] he treated practice as categorically separate from and subservient to the theory, principle or plan which 'guides' it.

Escaping this snare is no easy matter. It requires asserting that the practice of teachers is neither to be understood as the realisation of plans or proposals, nor as the application of principles derived from bodies of research. It requires asserting that the practice to be theorised in education or curriculum studies is not a universalised, abstracted 'practice-in-general' but the concrete, particular, material practice of each particular teacher working in her or his own particular site. It requires a whole-hearted embrace of the notion of practical reasoning[38]; it requires a whole-hearted embrace of the notion that theory and practice are dialectically related[39]; it requires rejecting the view that an adequate educational theory is one which generalises across settings even if it does not capture the idiosyncracies and fine-grained local variations of particular acts and sites of teaching and teachers[40]; and it requires rejecting as misleading the distinction between macro- and micro-settings, structures and theories (and even some usages of the distinction between the general and the particular).[41] Stenhouse's writings reflect a sympathy with some of these perspectives and even, in places, an equivocal or qualified support for them, but they are not fundamental to his thinking. If they were — that is, if he had fully grasped their implications — his writings would be other than they are.[42]

That Stenhouse was ambiguous on such matters is no more than an indication of his own intellectual history and preoccupations. There are different theoretical resources available today, and different frameworks from which to view the problems. But the problem of theory and practice endures, and he was correct to give it the emphasis he did: he was right to stress the improvement of practice through teacher research. We have different theoretical resources available to us, and we can make different resolutions of the issues — but it requires of us that we give up empiricist views of theory, technical and instrumentalist views of the functions of educational research, some old notions of generalisation, and some old views of the relationship between action in particular settings and the 'macro-theories' which might help us to explain or understand it. Given the empiricist, instrumentalist ideology of our culture and given our own intellectual histories, these habits of mind are hard to break.

Theory and practice versus knowledge and action

Despite his emphasis on theory as propositional and generalising, I believe that there are further ambiguities in Stenhouse's view of the relationship between theory and practice which can best be summarised in terms of a confusion between *theory and practice*, on the one hand, and (knowledge or) *thought and action*, on the other. This seems to me to be a common problem in discussions of the relationship between educational theory and practice.

There is an equivocation about what might be thought of as the 'public' and the 'private' realm in Stenhouse's views about research. There is more than a suggestion that research is 'public' when it contributes to the academic field of education (for example, appearing in learned journals), while the classroom is 'private'. He defined research in this way: 'Research is systematic enquiry made public. It is made public for criticism and utilisation within a particular research tradition . . .'[43] As Jean Rudduck points out,[44] however, he modified this notion, settling for 'systematic enquiry' as a way for teachers to improve their understandings of their practice. She quotes Stenhouse:

> The function of educational research in its application to practice is to provide a theory of educational practice testable by the experiments of teachers in classrooms. In a sense this calls for the development of the role of teacher as researcher, but only in a minimal sense. The basic desideratum is systematic enquiry; *it is not necessary that this enquiry be made public unless it offers a contribution to a public theory of education.* [my emphasis] [45]

One can see how a confusion about 'public' and 'private' realms might arise. For most teachers, including teachers of curriculum studies, theorising about education is something that occurs away from practice. It happens at sites and times other than the sites and times of practice itself. Our images of the sites of theorising are ones involving books and armchairs, or desks and blank sheets of paper; our expectations about the time for theorising are that it happens outside the hurly-burly of the teaching day. We nevertheless think about these sites and times of theorising as significant for practice. Retrospectively, they permit interpretation of practical puzzlements; prospectively, they promise guidance, perhaps even prescriptions for practice. My first point is that these images (misleadingly) suggest that theory is something 'outside' practice, or at least that theorising is not normally regarded as a central part of practising.

A second point is that many discussions of the relationship between theory and practice treat it *individualistically* — as a cognitive matter.[46] While using the language of theory and practice, they are actually concerned with the relationship between thought and action: the ways in which the conduct of practitioners is mediated by ideas. There is a growing literature of reflection which concerns itself with just this relationship between thought and action, given new impetus by Donald Schon's notion of the 'reflective practitioner'.[47] If theory and theorising are understood in terms of reflection, they seem to refer to aspects of cognitive functioning, including the relationship of ideas to action: how reflection expresses itself in the life and work of the practitioner. On this basis, we might speak of every practitioner as being guided by theory, meaning no more by this than that the practitioner has ideas. This seems to me to be an insufficient basis for asserting that a practitioner has a theory.

Instead, I would argue that thought (including beliefs) becomes knowledge,[48] and knowledge is accommodated in theory (thus gaining credibility as a claim to knowledge), by being tested, justified and sustained through a *social process* of debate. And when this debate is conducted in the light of shared values about truth and rationality (for example), it is itself a *social practice*. It seems to me that when we call this a 'public' process, we mean no more than that the debate is conducted as a social practice; if this is so, then the debate itself, and not necessarily the publication of findings meets the requirement of 'going public'.[49]

The testing and justifying of new ideas and insights is a process of theorising which establishes agreements and disagreements of new knowledge with what others know. By being reconciled with what others have already contributed to a common stock of knowledge, it is found a place in the (public) realm of theory. On this view, theoretical knowledge thus bears a different relationship to action from private knowledge. Theoretical knowledge is mediated not only through the minds of individuals but also through public processes in which actions come to be understood as practices, as activities of a certain type, whose meaning and significance is shared among groups of people, perhaps whole communities.

Thus, it seems to me, Stenhouse was correct in defining research as a public activity, and mistaken in modifying this strong view. The narrow view of the relationship between 'theory' (= thought) and 'practice' (= action) should be distinguished from the broader conception of the relationship between theory and practice which treats their relationship in terms of public processes. The relationship between theory and practice, on a strong view, must be understood in terms of the public sphere rather than the private (the mediation of thought and action in the life and work of an individual).

On the broader view, then, the mediation of theory and practice is a public process. It relates a common stock of theoretical ideas, understood in the framework of traditions[50] of thought, to theorised activities, regulated as practices (frequently within the structured framework of institutions). Exploring the mediation of theory and practice is, on this view, inevitably a public task, realised through social processes of research and evaluation — even if only in discussion in a school staff room.[51]

This view of the relationship between theory and practice involves a notion of *politics* — the politics of debate. For the philosopher Alasdair MacIntyre, the politics is liberal individualism, a debate in which individuals advance, defend, attack and counterattack arguments guided by different views of rationality and practical reasoning whose roots he traces back to Athens in the fifth and fourth centuries BC. An alternative to MacIntyre's view[52] is that of Habermas, whose view is based on a politics of discussion in which the conditions for rational discussion are those of democratic participation in discourse. Habermas describes the 'ideal speech situation' — note that he is describing an *ideal* speech situation, not the conditions of usual discourse in groups — necessary for a rational consensus:

... the design of an ideal speech situation is necessarily implied in the structure of potential speech, since all speech, even intentional deception, is oriented towards the idea of truth ... In so far as we master the means for the construction of the ideal speech situation, we conceive the ideas of truth, freedom and justice ...[53]

What is common to the different accounts of the politics of debate given by MacIntyre and Habermas is a sense that rationality does involve a politics — and that it is a public process of reclaiming and extending not merely meanings (for individuals) but also agreements between people reached on the basis of (public) argument. While MacIntyre emphasises the location of debate primarily in history and traditions (as debates extended through time), Habermas emphasises the location of debate in the contemporary social processes of real groups striving for consensus. Despite the substantial differences which divide them, there is some complementarity between them on this point.

In elaborating the politics of the process of debate, Habermas begins to identify those practices which (in his view) constitute rationality: the raising, challenging and redeeming of 'validity claims' which are, he argues, presupposed by all utterances. These are the implicit claims that what is spoken is (a) comprehensible, (b) true, (c) right or appropriate in a given situation, and (d) truthfully or sincerely stated. In discourse (a level of debate about what is being communicated), speakers explore the validity claims presupposed in their communication with one another. He goes on to argue that this kind of rationality is only possible in democratic contexts of open discussion.[54]

In his Humanities Curriculum Project mode, committed to the discussion of controversial issues, Stenhouse would probably have been generally sympathetic to this idea of rational discourse. His definition of research, and his modification of the idea of 'made public' suggests, however, that the final test is not discussion but publication. It would have been sufficient to take the view that research is a public activity when it is consciously and deliberately tested through critical discussion. This move retains the strong view of research as 'systematic enquiry made public', though widening the domain of what is to be regarded as making enquiries public. If this is accepted, it is nevertheless possible to reject as partial and misleading the cognitive view of the relationship between theory and practice (which confuses it with knowledge and action, as in the notion of the 'reflective practitioner'), and to assert not only that relating theory and practice to one another is a public process (a social practice), but also that it therefore involves a (practice of) politics.

Apart from leading to simple confusion, the equivocal use of the term 'theory' to apply sometimes to publicly justified knowledge, and sometimes to the ideas of individuals (without reference to a common source in tradition, culture or social processes and practices of communication) permits a dignification of unexamined ideas as 'theory'. This, in turn, permits equivocation about the location of (theoretically justified) practice in the social and historical tradition which gives it meaning and significance. It fractures practice from its social, cultural, historical and political grounding and thus permits — even fosters — a relativism (though disguising it as pluralism). This is a liberal individualist view which, though it accepts that consciousness defines reality, runs the risk of ignoring the insight that social reality also defines consciousness. Though part of a long tradition in social theory, this perspective is expounded and developed in Giddens' theory of agency and structure (to name just one source), and in his analysis of ideology.[55]

Educational theorists today cannot afford to ignore such insights if they are to make sense of how social practices (including educational practices) come to have the character they do, and if they are to help educational practitioners to see their practices within the wider social and historical frames that give them meaning and significance. When these wider frames are ignored, the very concept of 'practice' is devalued, making it barely distinguishable from 'action' or even 'behaviour'. In this demeaned sense, it risks having meaning and significance attributed to it by external agencies and authorities; it risks being treated as the 'property' of employers, including ministers or secretaries of state for education and other educational administrators — a technical activity to be guided by policy rather than theory. As seems to be happening in contemporary Britain, accepting this demeaned understanding of practice permits the control of education by 'policy-makers', and permits them to control what goes on in schools without reference to the knowledge of individual teachers, without reference to educational theories currently being developed by teachers and other educational researchers, without reference to the traditions of educational theory or educational practice, and without reference to the wider democratic traditions of a democratic society. Perhaps rehabilitating the concept of practice would make a small contribution to the permanent struggle to make schooling educational. If this is so, it would be a contribution of which Stenhouse would certainly have approved.

The division of labour between academic theorists and classroom practitioners

A further ambiguity in Stenhouse's work concerns the relationship between academic educational researchers and classroom researcher-practitioners. Clearly, he wanted teachers to be active as researchers into their own practices, and clearly he wanted to establish a tradition of research-based teaching.[56] He was not overambitious or unrealistic in this advocacy, however: he believed that it might be a generation or more before teachers could 'possess this field of research' for themselves — and it is not clear how seriously he took this as an ultimate

objective. He was a realist about the power of academic educational researchers
— he accepted that they had a role in the development of educational theory and
in making proposals for the continuing improvement of practice. On the one hand,
he believed that academic researchers should be more concerned about the practical
exigencies of classrooms[57]; on the other hand, he believed that educational theory
should be built on the foundations of critically examined classroom practice[58]
(including archives of case records and case studies of practice). He certainly
believed that the relationship between academic theorists and classroom
practitioners should be based on greater courtesy and mutual respect.

In some ways, Stenhouse may have been hampered in his thinking about the
relationship between theory and practice because he focused too sharply on the
roles of 'theorist' and 'practitioner'. For most of us, it is not just that the sites
and times of theorising are separated from sites and times of practice; theorising
and practising are also separated in the larger social framework by the division
of labour and differentiation of function in the institutional structures of
contemporary schooling. There are people whose primary tasks are understood
to be theorising (academic educational researchers, for example), and others
(teachers) whose primary tasks are practice. True, the 'official' theorists may
also be practitioners for some of their time, and the 'official' pracitioners may
also sometimes be theorists, but we have come to expect that the primary
responsibilities of each are distinctive.

Once we have accepted that there is a *technical division of labour* between
theorising and practising (as is suggested by the empiricist, rationalist view of
theory), then it is but a short step to accepting a *social division of labour* between
theorists and practitioners (an alleged differentiation of functions leading to the
differentiation of roles). The we can suppose that the theorist makes a contribution
to education from the library, the laboratory, the desk or the podium; the
practitioner in face-to-face interaction with students. It seems that, in the overall
division of labour of education, we have our own version of the distinction between
mental and manual work, and between white-collar and blue-collar workers; it
seems that, in the broad institutional structure of education, we have our own
distinctions between the business office and the factory floor.

The analysis of theory and practice in terms of roles soon becomes muddied,
however, when we think about the complex of relationships between (so-called)
theorists' theories and practices and (so-called) practitioners' theories and practices.
We need to be clear about exactly what (and whose) practices and what (and whose)
theories are being considered at any time. As already suggested, people do not stay
neatly in role: at times, setting aside the role of practitioner of theorising, the
educational theorist is a practitioner of education (a teacher); at times the teacher
(as educational practitioner) is a theorist. And there are further complexities: it

may be that theorists' theories are usually aimed at explaining or interpreting practitioners' practices, or even at explaining or interpreting practitioners' theories; in general, however, educational theorists have given less attention to explaining their own theories of their own educational (or teaching) practices.[59] Moreover, despite the vast literature of idealised research methodology, there is also a reluctance among educational theorists to theorise their practice of theorising as a lived experience or as a form of work.[60] Though related, the different, institutionally separated practices of educational theorising and teaching may need different theories to explain, interpret or justify them.

Such an analysis, beginning from roles, can help us to clarify just what practices are being theorised, when and by whom. From this beginning, we can make a more robust analysis of the processes of theorising and practising. When we are clear about just what practices (or what theories) are the focus of our analysis, however, we discover that the particular practices we are interested in cannot be understood except by reference to the theories that they embody, that give them meaning and significance. We discover that theory and practice cannot be separated. As Carr and Kemmis have argued,[61] it is by being theorised that practices have meaning (as practices of a certain kind), and it is by being practised that theories have historical, social and material significance and consequences. Theory is not just words, and practice is not mute behaviour; theory and practice are mutually constitutive. On this view, there can be no 'gap' between theory and practice, only greater and lesser degrees of mismatch, elision and illusion in the relationship between them. We can only identify these mismatches, elisions, and illusions by examining how our theories and practices interrelate. Moreover, practices of theorising education (on the one hand) and practices of education (on the other) *are themselves related through practices*. They are related through human and social activities which understand themselves to be related to theory — for example, the application of theory, or the decision to act in a certain way on the basis of a certain perspective or, at their best, through the public processes — the practices — of critical reflection and self-reflection.

In drawing attention to the relationship between teachers and researchers in terms of (possibly co-operative, too often dissociated) roles, Stenhouse rightly draws attention to the power relationships between teachers and academic researchers. Here again, he was on the brink of major developments in contemporary social theory. Without stretching the point too far, perhaps he was searching for a version of Foucault's notion of power/knowledge.[62] In the distinction between academic educational theory and teacher enquiry, Stenhouse was aware of the significance of the practices of educational researchers who give order[63] to knowledge from their places in the academy (or, increasingly, in the service of state education authorities) — and aware of the relative power of teachers when it comes to the ordering of their professional knowledge and their professional work. Foucault persuasively argues that 'discipline' is a double-sided concept: on the one side, it refers an ordering of knowledge, and, on the other, to an ordering of people and their work.[64] Schools as mass institutions arose alongside hospitals, workhouses and the police; they still perform the functions of establishing an order, a discipline, for the state. It is hardly necessary to point out the affinities between contemporary British national curriculum development and testing and the disciplinary order and surveillance of the eighteenth century hospitals of which Foucalt wrote:

> The keeping of registers, nurse specification, the modes of transcription from one to the other, their circulation during visits, their comparison during regular meetings of doctors and administrators, the transmission of the data to centralising bodies (either at the hospital or at the central office of the poorhouses), the accountancy of diseases, cures, deaths, at the level of a hospital, a town and even of the nation as a whole formed an integral part of the process by which hospitals were subjected to the disciplinary regime. Among the fundamental conditions of a good medical 'discipline', in both senses of the word, one must include the procedures of writing that made it possible to integrate individual data into cumulative systems in such a way that they were not lost; so to arrange things that an individual could be located in the general register . . .[65]

Nor, perhaps, would it be irrelevant in the contemporary British context to consider Foucault's views on the reform of penal institutions and the role of the people who live and work in those institutions in bringing about reform:

> If prisons and punitive mechanisms are transformed, it won't be because a plan of reform has found its way into the heads of the social workers; it will be when those who have to do with that penal reality, all those people, have come into collision with each other and themselves, run into dead ends, problems and impossibilities, been through conflicts and confrontations; when critique has been played out in the real, not when reformers have realised their ideals . . .
>
> Critique does not have to be the premise of a deduction which concludes: this then is what needs to be done. It should be an instrument for those who fight, those who refuse and resist what is. Its use should be in processes of conflict and confrontation, essays in refusal.[66]

Similarly, it might be argued, schools will not be transformed until those who work in them have 'come into collision . . . , run into dead ends, problems and possibilities . . .' and until their 'essays in refusal' make schools otherwise. To put it another way: schools will be transformed when those who live and work in them constitute their work in other ways — when their practices are other practices, which, by running against the grain of the existing modes of order and organisation of the institution, cause the institution to become something other than it is, an institution of another kind. This would be no new thing: major transformations of this kind have happened many times before in the history of education (like the transformation of the practices of schooling under the influence of the industrial revolution and the development of factory production), and minor transformations occur each day in different ways, as students and teachers give their working relationships a distinctive stamp. The 'essays of refusal' of teachers who want to sustain educational relationships with students, and of students who resist being integrated within the bureaucratic forms and disciplines of schooling are constantly and spontaneously generating new practices and changing the character of schools as institutions. At the same time, new policies, procedures, patterns of accountability and control are reconstituting the practice and the institutions of schooling in other ways, rationalising and integrating practice within the cultural, economic and political systems of the wider society.

Academic educational researchers relate to these spontaneous, counter-hegemonic forms and to the system-integrative, hegemonic forms of reconstitution of practice in contradictory ways. Academic educational researchers are them-selves, as teachers and as researchers, increasingly subject to state discipline and co-opted by funding and other arrangements to closer state control. On the one hand, many resist the instrumentalisation and rationalisation of their own teaching, yet through their research, they play a system-integrative role with respect to the work of teachers in schools. In their research, they are like Foucalt's social workers with plans of reform in their heads, aiding and abetting system integration; in their teaching (their school reality), they try to live out their essays of refusal, playing out critique in the real. These contradictions can only be sustained by drawing divisions beween research and teaching, seeing them as different modes of work guided by different kinds of theories and different kinds of values, denying the connections between them. Yet academic educational researchers and class-room teachers are connected by their work, their discourse and their educational values. Overcoming the contradictions between research and teaching seems to me to be a pressing task for educational researchers and educational research associa-tions — and for teachers. It is a pressing task not only so we can overcome the contradictions for our own sakes, within our own practices, but also, for the sake of education, so we can overcome the contradictions in the wider social practices that connect us to other teachers, maintaining and transforming the interrelation-ships between educational institutions and thus maintaining or transforming the culture, the economies and the politics of the societies in which we live.

The times have changed since Lawrence Stenhouse's death. He wanted researchers to have their feet on the ground in working with teachers. Words like Foucault's were not his style, even if there might have been some common ground between them. It seems to me, though, that the present circumstances of education in Britain may well have given him reason for words just as forthright, and driven him to forge even closer alliances with teachers against the conditions of curriculum development and curriculum control in Britain today.[67]

The politics of change: Professionals, the social order and social movements

Yes: times have changed. Britain ten years ago, fifteen years ago, seemed to me a kinder, more liberal place. Stenhouse's voice was an eloquent expression of those times. And, in 1975, his words reflect a faith in the institutions of education — a taken-for-grantedness of the civilised value of the institutions — which nowadays might sound naive, even, perhaps, conservative. Listen:

> The power of the individual teacher is limited. Without his strengths the betterment of schools can never be achieved; but the strengths of individuals are not effective unless they are co-ordinated and supported. The primary unit of co-ordination and support is the school.[68]

> We have in Britain a wide range of supporting agencies: Her Majesty's Inspectorate, local advisory services, teachers' centres, research and development units, in-service training agencies and initial training institutions. It is my thesis that they and the schools should be united in a common research and development tradition.[69]

> Responsibility [for action towards betterment of curriculum and teaching] lies with local authorities, schools and teachers. Among those who carry that responsibility there will be those who incline to system maintenance and those who are dedicated to bettering the situation. The balance of power between them will depend upon either criteria or appointment or the way people respond to their gradual assessment of their power and how it can be used after they have been appointed. Those who are professionally concerned with research and development can do no more than collaborate with those in the action setting who want to improve things and perhaps make improvement a more attractive and practicable policy, as compared with system maintenance, to those teachers and administrators who do not have a determined policy commitment.[70]

These words express faith in a generally liberal, progressive social order, and suggest that the social order has sufficient resources for liberal, progressive reform. The formation of alliances within the social order is Stenhouse's basic strategy for reform: 'alliance to those who, having direct power in the system, wish to pursue policies of improvement, and those who have the power through research and development to support those actors'.[71] Of course, such alliances remain necessary, but perhaps there is a need to be more judicious these days in choosing allies.

As against the improvement of education through the system, the social order, Stenhouse has next to no faith in social movements. In *An Introduction to Curriculum Research and Development*, he sees movements as an inadequate basis for the systematic improvement of education. After a discussion of Cremin's[72] analysis of the failure of the progressive movement, Stenhouse concludes:

> At the root of the failure of a movement there seem to me to be two linked weaknesses: an insistence on 'hearts, not heads', and the lack of a public tradition of improvement by systematic self-criticism.[73]

This tradition of 'systematic self-criticism' could be developed through teacher research:

> ... the emergence of a healthy tradition of curriculum research and development depends upon a partnership of teachers and curriculum research workers. And such a partnership depends upon the sharing of this tradition. The development must be through co-operation and towards a more solid basis for that co-operation.
>
> The key factor would seem to be the induction of teachers into such a tradition in the course of initial training and the accessibility of the tradition to experienced teachers through in-service education. Research workers have a contribution to make; but it is the teachers who in the end will change the world of the school by understanding it.[74]

It is clear from these quotations that Stenhouse believed the tradition of teacher research should avoid becoming a 'movement' and that it should be incorporated into the social ordering of education systems. Indeed, he wrote scathingly:

> It is one of the problems of research and development in curriculum that it is continually threatening to turn into the Curriculum Development Movement. If those of us who are interested in the improvement of schools by research — that is, by reflective questioning and constructive criticism — are to avoid this fate, we must address ourselves to heads as well as hearts, we must deal in hypotheses rather than slogans, we must ensure that theory is about practice and we must ensure that techniques are developed to match aspirations.[75]

In short, Stenhouse appeared to associate movements with 'hearts, not heads' and sloganising, and the development of a tradition with 'heads as well as hearts' and the testing of hypotheses in practice. Movements were suspect because they lack a 'solid base'; the development of a research tradition depended on alliance and support from authorities and agencies within systems.[76]

I think Stenhouse was mistaken about these connections. He saw social movement and social order as alternatives, not as permanently locked in productive, dialectical tension.[77] Alain Touraine,[78] by contrast, explores the tension between social order and social movement as a basis for explaining processes of social change and reform. Indeed, Touraine identifies social movements as a primary means contributing to the self-production of society through the struggle with existing social order. Touraine's examples include the workers' movement, the green movement and the women's movement. Through examining such movements, he shows how contestation within and against the mechanisms of social order generates transformations in society.

This approach to the relationship between social order and social movement seems to me to be significant in understanding educational change and reform, especially in relation to the role of teachers' professional organisations and unions. As the experience of the Victorian Secondary Teachers' Association in Australia through the 1970s and early 1980s shows, teachers' professional organisations can provide a critical and constructive reading of the effects of existing policies and structures, and industrial-political action by teachers can bring about substantial and worthwhile educational reform — based not on dogma or slogans, but on a research-based analysis and experimentation directed at curriculum, pedagogy and the institutional structures of education.

My reading of Stenhouse on social order and social movement and the role of the profession, then, is that he underestimates the significance and the power of social movements, and that he places too great a faith in the commitment of the educational order to changing itself. His notion of 'systematic self-criticism', seen in this light, seems to me to be double-sided in the same way as Foucault's notion of 'discipline': it is 'systematic' both in the sense that it is 'within the system', and in the sense that it is to be a means of 'systematising' not only the research act but also the acts of teaching. In this, as in other ways, Stenhouse may have reflected his times; educational researchers today might draw different conclusions about social order and social movement, and consequently form their 'alliances' with state education officials and with teachers somewhat differently from the ways Stenhouse envisaged.

In discussing the ambiguities of Stenhouse's views of theory and its relation to practice, the possible confusion of 'theory and practice' with 'knowledge and action', the division of labour between teachers and academic educational researchers, and the relationship between social order and social movements, I have attempted to show that Stenhouse was a man of his time, but nevertheless a transitional figure, dealing with important problems. I have also tried to show, by reference to theoretical resources not available or readily available to him, that some of his ways of dealing with the issues prevented him from resolving them more adequately. I have also tried to show that the problems continue to confront us today, and that they pose continuing challenges to contemporary educational researchers. In the light of the metatheoretical resources available to us, perhaps we can reach more adequate resolutions.

Towards a New Resolution: Metatheory and Metapractice

The nature of educational practice has been the object of increasingly close analysis of various kinds over the last hundred years. In some phases, it has been theorised in the tradition of the humanities, as an expression of educational values thought central to the development of a progressive, enlightened and educative society; in other phases, it has been theorised in the tradition of the physical sciences, using resources drawn from disciplines outside education. The recovery of 'metatheory' – the theory of theory – in educational theorising and research has made it possible to form new perspectives on educational research and theorising,[79] and has led to new developments in educational theory and approaches to educational research.

Despite these developments, however, educational practice has not yet succeeded in freeing itself from the irrationalities and constraints which have reduced contemporary schooling, at worst, to an instrumental function of service to economic and social ends which, while functional from the perspective of the economy, may yet turn out to be anti-educational. This contradictory state of affairs has arisen despite new forms of educational theorising and educational research; it has arisen not as a consequence of ways of viewing education but as a result of practices external to schools which constrain and increasingly control them. Though (metatheoretical) ways of viewing the world of education offer us the alternative prospects of education increasingly bound to the imperatives of industry and the state, or education able to fulfil traditional values of individual enlightenment and social emancipation, it is not just by developing different ways of viewing the world that we can remake it; in addition, we need alternative forms of practice which will allow us to make it otherwise.

Stenhouse understood this point. He aimed to develop an alternative tradition of educational research which would give teachers a central role in the development of educational theory, and to develop a new tradition in the relationship between teachers and academic educational researchers. He wanted teaching to be research-based, and he wanted educational researchers to work co-operatively with teachers. He was calling for different *practices* of educational research, and different practices in the relationships between teachers and academic educational researchers.

As far as I can see, Stenhouse was interested in, but not much compelled by, the recovery of metatheory in social and educational research.[80]

As I have suggested earlier, I think this prevented him from finding new ways to resolve the problem of the relationships beween theory and practice and theorists and practitioners. But there is no doubt that he was interested in practice; in so far as he was interested in theory as a source of justification for educational practice, and in educational policy as a means for controlling practice, I would want to argue that he evinced a strong interest in the forms of *research practice* which help to constitute and which frequently function to constrain *educational practice* in schools and classrooms. In what follows, I will describe these research practices which constitute and constrain educational practice as *metapractices*.

The species of practices which might be described as 'metapractices' earn the prefix 'meta-' by analogy with 'metatheories': just as metatheories are theories of theory, metapractices are social practices which structure, constrain and constitute the conditions for other practices. Metapractice may be conceived as a realm of practice in which the material practices and social relations of education are pre-formed and pre-structured for educational practitioners. In education, a variety of 'metapractices' function to constitute the conditions for educational practice in schools; they include not only practices of educational research, but also practices of educational administration and curriculum development (of which educational research is frequently a part). I want to argue that a reconstruction of these metapractices — and in particular the metapractice of educational research — is necessary for the improvement of schools, curriculum and the practices which constitute education.

We might define social (cultural, economic and political) reproduction as the production in the consciousness and social relationships of rising generations of particular kinds of existing knowledge, skills, activity and social orientations necessary for production. Social transformation by contrast, consists in the production of changed knowledge, skills and social orientations as a basis for changed modes of production. Similarly, we might define metapractices as including *those practices which produce particular processes of reproduction and transformation through the production of particular views of education in the consciousness of individuals, the production of particular material practices of education, and the production of particular kinds of social relationships between educational practitioners and others.*

Metapractices are thus ideological in character: just as one element of the concept of ideology is a notion of 'false consciousness', and another is the mobilisation of structures of signification to legitimate the sectional interests of hegemonic groups,[81] so metapractices function to reproduce certain forms of consciousness and to structure patterns of educational life and work in the interests of particular groups. Or, to put it another way, metapractice is a kind of analogue of the 'hidden' curriculum experienced by students: a 'hidden curriculum' about the nature of education for educational practitioners.

Though the development of metatheoretical perspectives on the relationship between theory and practice in education has produced valuable and important insights into the nature of the relationship between theory and practice, and the development of practical and critical forms of educational research on the basis of these metatheoretical perspectives have produced important results in changing the metapractices by which research relates to educational practice, we still have far to go in comprehending the implications of metatheory for the conduct of educational research. As a way forward, it seems to me that the notion of metatheory must be given a historical materialist foundation in the work of educational practitioners and others whose work is intended to support (though often implicitly denies) the development of educational practice.

The practical, concrete, material character of metapractice must be emphasised. The problems of contemporary education (for example, its instrumentalisation to economic demands) are not just problems of wrong ways of viewing the world (having wrong metatheories, for example), they are problems because of their material and historical consequences, and these consequence are the consequences of our practices — the consequences of what we do (including what we say) and how we do it. Practical problems of education, like its instrumentalisation to economic demands, arise as a consequence of the material practices and social relationships through which the relationships between educational theory, policy and practice are lived — how they are concretely constituted in particular places at particular moments in history.

Educational research is frequently implicated in the creation of circumstances under which these problems of education arise. For example, service research and evaluation for education authorities may create conditions under which education is more securely harnessed to the economy (for example, in relation to such programmes as the Technical Vocational Education Initiative), and even practices of self-evaluation, using techniques from educational research (including educational action research), may yoke teacheres to an increasingly managerial and technicist system of state control of education. But there is no necessity that the work of research and the work of teaching should be linked in this way; indeed, other means and modes of research production could produce other kinds of educational practice in schools. Thus, it seems to me, some contemporary problems of education can be addressed, perhaps even resolved, by adopting different metapractices in the relation of educational research to educational practice: allowing educational practice to be constituted and legitimated in different ways. On this point, at least, I think Stenhouse would agree.

The appropriation of educational theory as a specialist activity (of 'theorists' and 'researchers') is a consequence of a differentiation of function which has been institutionalised in a division of labour between theorists and practitioners. [82] The consequences of this division of labour can be read not only in the practices of educational theorising and research, but also in the nature of certain educational conferences, in teacher education, in the work of curriculum development, and in the practical relationships which underpin the work of educational policy-makers vis-à-vis educational practitioners, that is, *in the working relationships between educational theorists and educational practitioners.* These working relationships can be described in terms of metapractice — they are among the relationships which constitute educational practice in classrooms and schools.

Moreover, in the historical development of education, especially since the rise of mass education, the control of educational practice has shifted from the sites of education itself to certain sites (of curriculum development, educational policy-making and administration) physically and socially removed from the sites of educational practice. The historically evolving material practices and social relationships of educational research — the different metapractices of educational research — have different and particular social and political characters within the overall control of education, sometimes as a source of legitimation of practices, sometimes producing new and better justified forms of educational practice. At every stage, however, these patterns produce different and particular material and historical consequences. Examples include: the work of Cyril Burt in the development of the 1944 Education Act in England and Wales (producing the differentiation between grammar and secondary modern schools); the work of Neville Bennett and his colleagues in the debate over formal versus informal teaching styles; the work of independent evaluators in curriculum development projects and educational reform programs[83]; the work of the project team vis-à-vis teachers in Stenhouse's Humanities Curriculum Project or in his work on the problems of teaching about race relations; the work of university and college-based researcher–facilitators in various action research projects; and the work of teacher researchers working together in a region on issues of common interest — each with different, and sometimes massive, social and educational implications and ramifications.

When educational research is allied with and integrated into state agencies of education, as is increasingly the case throughout the Western world, however, the consequences of these working relationships may even, at times, include the destruction of educational values. Under contemporary circumstances, for example, educational research frequently plays a role in decontextualising, abstracting, reifying the concrete processes and practices of education, and in standardising, legitimating and ideologically reconstructing educational practice within frameworks of values and interests external to the values and interests of education — the values and purposes which have traditionally given the practice of education its meaning and significance.[84] In short, the development of educational research has played, and continues to play, a constituting and constraining role within the wider history of education, and *the traditions of educational research may thus be read in terms of historically developed and developing metapractices which establish different patterns of working relationships between researchers and practitioners, producing different patterns of consequences for both.*

In proposing the concept of metapractice, I am trying to say more than that educational research is ideological — by now a truism to anyone with more than a passing acquaintance with the concept of ideology. I am wanting to assert that it has its specific ideological character *as a matter of practice*. And I want to use the notion to draw attention to the need to reconstruct the working relationships between educational theorising and educational practice — the work of educational research.

I believe that the concept of metapractice can help to resolve some of the problems of Stenhouse's views of theory and its relationship to practice, the individual and public processes of research, the division of labour between theorists and practitioners, and the connections between social order, social movement and the profession — that is, the problems discussed in the earlier, critical section of this chapter. As I have described it, the concept of metapractice refers simultaneously to: (1) theorising and research as concrete, material practices aimed at constituting or reconstituting educational practices; (2) the processes of communication, production and social organisation by which both educational research and educational practice are constituted and reconstituted; (3) the actual social relationships among and between educational researchers and educational practitioners; and (4) the practical (ideological) connections between educational researchers and practitioners and the sectional interests of hegemonic groups (the location of researchers and practitioners in relation to the social order and social movements.

Stenhouse had already put the question of the relationship between theory and practice on a concrete footing (the working relationship between researchers and practitioners). He was hampered in making greater progress in his (negative) attack on much conventional educational research and in his (positive) advocacy of teacher research by such views as his empiricist, rationalistic understanding of theory, his equivocal use of 'theory' sometimes to refer to teachers' knowledge or thought, and his misunderstanding of the mutually constitutive relationship between social order and social movement in the processes of educational innovation and reform. A metapractical analysis of the working relationships between educational research and educational practice can overcome some of these problems. In particular, specific metapractical analyses of specific working relationships between educational research and educational practice can help to avoid the problem of reifying the relationship in terms of the social order — and especially the problems of Stenhouse's views about educational research which overidentify:

(1) the movement from particular to general propositions with
(2) the movement from private experience to public knowledge with
(3) the movement from local to universal settings or locations with
(4) the movement from individual teachers, classrooms and schools to education systems (the social order in education).

These problems, in my view, are at the heart of the issue about the relationship between educational theory, research and practice, and they are problems which still bedevil much educational research and theorising. They are problems that remain with us today.

An example of Metapractice: Educational Research and the Educational Conference

There is nothing unfamiliar these days about questions of the 'ethics' and 'principles of procedure' of educational research and evaluation. Researchers and evaluators from the Centre for Applied Research in Education at the University of East Anglia have written extensively on the topic.[85] These authors have concerned themselves with questions such as: 'Who owns the data?' 'Who gets to decide on the validity of interpretations?' 'What kinds of data yield what kinds of perspectives on educational settings?' They saw the conduct of research and evaluation in terms of the construction of political economies of information, leading, in general, to questions of 'Who gets to know what about whom?'

As was suggested early on by such authors as Parsons[86] and Reynolds,[87] however, there was still a problem of assimilating these views of 'ethics' and 'principles', as well as the general question of the political economy of information in educational research and evaluation, to a wider social theory which might explain them as well as making moral or political claims about them. Habermas's theory of knowledge-constitutive interests[88] seemed to me to offer one way of reconciling these concerns to social theory,[89] though there has been a good deal of debate about the success of Habermas's theory.[90]

There is a deep-seated problem of understanding, explaining or justifying how specific research and evaluation studies create patterns of working relationships between researchers (or evaluators), teachers and others. The problem concerns the way in which the particular circumstances of particular studies can be reconciled with any general social theory. As Giddens has shown,[91] this *cannot* be achieved as a relationship of 'micro' to 'macro' studies; the distinction itself is misleading. What is needed instead (and Giddens's theory of agency and structure offers one way of achieving it) is a more dialectical form of analysis which allows the general to be seen *in* the particular and the particular *in* the general. For this, a theory of social practice like that of Giddens becomes necessary.

I cannot attempt to outline such a theory here. I can do no more than to emphasise that questions of legitimation, domination, and social and system integration (for example) are not merely questions of 'rights' or questions of 'control'. There is a naive view of power which rests content with 'unmasking' the coercive and hierarchical character of power relations in social and educational settings, including the settings of educational research, as if, once the power relationship had been 'unmasked', people could do something to change them. These theories are frequently poor on suggesting any 'solution' to the problem other than that open and equal power relations between actors should be created[92] — an ideal state never reached in social life, and arguably not even desirable in the day-to-day conduct of (social and) educational affairs in (social and) educational institutions. A *relational* view of power, and, more importantly still, a *substantive relational* view of power is necessary. For this, such theorists as Foucault and Giddens provide the theoretical means.[93] A substantive relational view of power permits an analysis of how the means and modes of production in educational research involve concrete, material practices which forge specific, substantive kinds of relations between researchers, those researched and others; it permits an analysis of how specific, substantive forms of disciplinary knowledge (in Foucault's two senses) arise from or are reinforced through particular research studies; and it permits an analysis of how these relationships and disciplinary orders are connected to particular patterns of material and social consequences. To put it in Foucault's terms, it permits us to interrelate technologies of power, programmes of ideas, strategies, and effects. In what follows, I will suggest just a few places to look to discover the substantive character and consequences of the working relationships forged in educational research, and thus provide some examples of metapractices.

Consider the example of an educational research conference. It provides evidence about the working relationships between academic researchers and classroom practitioners both through the content of the papers presented and through the forms of work which bring participants together, order their conduct at the conference, and connect them in different ways to others not present. Such an analysis reveals a vast array of detailed metapractices of educational research. We might ask, for example:

Who is present? What work do they report? Whose work is described in the papers presented? Whose interests are served in the process of reporting (and how far are these the interests of the researcher, the researched and/or funding agencies or others involved in or affected by the research)? Who has read the report before it appears, and whose perspectives does it present? Whose views have been excluded?

What are the material practices of data-gathering in the research being reported? To what kinds of matter are they sensitive, and to what kinds of matters are they insensitive? How do they represent the life and work of education? How are they permeated by the values and interests of particular groups?

Is the report solely for the audience of the conference? How will the paper be circulated more widely beyond the group of people present? Who else will receive a copy of the paper after reading about it in the programme or in reports of the conference?

How does the substance of the work reported affect the work of those who hear the paper presented? Do they change their views about the nature of what they are studying themselves? Do they change their data-gathering methods? Are there people present who change their own educational practices as a consequence of what they hear? Who are they, and why do these people (and not others) change?

How does the reception of the report change the work being done by the presenter? What substantive arguments are offered, heard and/or acted upon? Why these arguments? What programmes of in-service education will be affected by the work reported? What classroom practices will in fact be changed?

A list of further questions could be added. My point is this: in the work of an educational conference, certain substantive working relationships and non-relationships between educational researchers and educational practitioners are being reported. These working relationships are metapractical — they are among the conditions which constitute and constrain the practices of education. But the conference papers do not only present retrospective accounts of metapractices; the work of the conference, the presentation and reception of the reports and the content of discussions and relationships is also prospective — it is metapractical in the sense that it creates conditions for the constitution and constraint of future educational practice. To greater and lesser degrees, it both reproduces and transforms existing practices (of research and teaching), existing working relationships, and existing modes of discourse.

The metapractices of the educational research conference can be analysed in terms of (say) Althusser's definition of a practice:

> By practice in general I shall mean any process of transformation of a determinate given raw material into a determinate product, a transformation effected by determinate human labour, using determinate means [of production].[94]

Using this notion of practice, we can examine the working relationships represented in the papers at the conference, the working relationships within the conference, and the working relationships prefigured by the conference — the relationships between the work of the conference and the work of educational practice it aims (rhetorically at least) to transform. Within the papers presented, we could examine, for example,

- the *determinate 'raw material'* (perhaps the work of teachers or schools as represented through questionnaire data, or interviews, or reviews of literature, or archival research)

- which is being 'processed' through *particular determinate means of production* (for example, particular statistical treatments, interpretive methods, or forms of critical analysis, and particular means of report writing and compilation)
- and *particular determinate modes of production* (including particular patterns of relationship between those whose work is the object of study, those doing the data-gathering, the analysis and the report-writing, those to whom the researchers are responsible, and the various audiences, present and not present, for the presentation of the paper),
- generating *particular determinate products* (reports of a particular style and content, and for particular audiences)
- with *particular determinate consequences* (for example, better ways of learning for some students, better ways of teaching for some teachers, a promotion for the presenter, new 'tricks of the trade' for a young researcher, new alliances and patterns of opposition between groups present, new alliances and oppositions between those present and not present, more/less funds for particular activities, more/less credibility for particular research and educational workers and their work, and so on)
- which serve *different, particular sectional interests differentially* (for example, the different self-interests of the researcher, of particular students in schools, particular teachers, parents, educational administrators, and other researchers; or, for example, the interests of men versus women, ethnic majorities versus minorities, ruling class versus working-class people and so on).

Each paper presented represents a web of working relationships, of metapractices.

In addition, we could use the Althusserian categories to analyse the work of the conference as a whole, to examine the extent to which the conference reproduces or transforms existing research and teaching practices, working relationships, and modes of discourse both among those present and in connection to others not present: the whole web of working relationships between educational researchers and educational practitioners. The working relationships within the conference and between the conferees and others not present reveal still further metapractices. Will there be practitioners whose working conditions change as a consequence of any of the papers presented here — but without their knowing where the 'new ideas' came from? Will there be students whose educational prospects will improve or deteriorate as a consequence of the proceedings? Who listens to (and who cares about) the proceedings of the conference?

Apart from those present at the conference, perhaps it will be the colleagues of those present and the administrators to whom they are responsible who will be most interested in what goes on. Perhaps a small number of people in a variety of different and specific locations will be affected. But perhaps the conference will serve most to confirm and reproduce, rather than to transform, the existing substantive and power relations of the sites and settings in which the research occurs. It may be a means of integrating those present (and others involved in the work reported) to the system of social relations which characterise institutionalised education, educational administration and educational research. Most likely, the work reported at the conference will function most powerfully to confirm the bureaucratic relations and modes of consciousness of those settings, the gendered relations of those settings, the class relations of those settings, and so on. Far from changing reality in order to understand or improve it, the overall effect of the conference may well be to affirm understandings of, and practices within those settings — that is, the effect of the conference will be to reproduce rather than transform the consciousness, practices and social relationships which characterise those settings.

Perhaps this is 'normal science'. Perhaps it is human nature. Perhaps it is hegemony at work. Perhaps it is a means by which the reproduction of certain ideological relationships of education and educational administration are ensured. Perhaps the work reported at educational research conferences helps to secure the mask of false consciousness and domination which permits us to continue in our work as educational researchers despite our failures to transform the educational reality of students, teachers, school communities and whole societies. Perhaps the conference is a ritual which secures not only the work of those who come but also, and more importantly, the educational practice of those whose work is *not* reported upon and those whose work is not even studied.

Of course, work will also be presented at the conference which challenges existing structures, expresses opposition, generates resistance, and fosters social movement. From a perspective outside the conference; some of this will be seen merely as 'letting off steam'. That is, a number of these critical contributions will be repressively tolerated. Though talk is a form of practice, and talk shapes and reshapes ways of orienting in the world, it is not a substitute for changing the material practices of educational research and educational practice. The conference is a political forum in which alliances and practices can be changed (or secured against the possibility of change), not only ways of seeing.

Yet few conferences conduct their business in order to generate systematic changes in the social relationships and material practices of educational research — let alone the social relationships and material practices of educational practice in schools and classrooms. The theory of change implied in most conferences is a liberal individualist theory — some people will be convinced of some things, and will go away from the conference committed to acting differently in one way or another. Many of the people involved in educational conferences reject liberal individualist perspectives in their political views, yet this is the foundation of their conference practice. They suspect that resolutions, declarations and manifestos are mere talk, and that the reaching of joint resolutions about action (either in the conference as a whole or in smaller groups) would be no more than a hollow gesture that few would feel bound by, yet, in other contexts, they would describe this reaction as a symptom of alienation and disempowerment, an expression of an individualism in the culture which has reached pathological levels.

In such ways, we who attend educational research conferences express our scepticism about the possibilities for transformation, our lack of resolution about our own work and our own world, let alone the work and world of teachers. Yet these working relationships — and the metapractices that give them substance and force — are the material stuff of our connectedness to practice. They are what we do research for; they are the means by which we can 'investigate reality in order to transform it' [95] and transform reality in order to understand it.

Such metapractices as these are the ones we must change if we are to change the practical relationship between our educational research and the work of education in schools and classrooms.

Conclusion: Reconstructing the Metapractices of Educational Research

The connections between educational research and educational practice, and the working relationships between academic educational researchers and classroom practitioners were the connections and working relationships Lawrence Stenhouse wanted to change.

I have tried to show how some of his views on these matters were ambiguous, and that there are now theoretical resources available which make it possible to see the problems he addressed differently, and perhaps more clearly. I have tried to show that the connections between research and practice, and between educational researchers and practitioners are practical connections: they are conducted in and through concrete, material practices which I have referred to as metapractices. I have tried to show that an analysis of the metapractices of educational research, for example, the metapractices revealed by an educational research conference, allows us to grasp the relationships between theory and practice not as matters of principle, nor even as matters of metatheory, but as quite concrete, practical, ordinary, everyday connections and relationships between the work of teachers and the work of researchers.

Perhaps, using a concept like that of metapractice, educational researchers can recover a sense of the intimacy and the practicality of the connections between their work and the work of teachers in classrooms and schools — not as questions of high moral principle (though principles remain relevant), political philosophy or epistemology, but as personal and practical political questions, as matters of work and working relationships. When we do so, I believe, we locate educational research not outside or alongside educational practice, but as part of a far wider web of social connections and relations. Then we may see educational research *within* educational practice, and educational theory *within* wider social theory. Most importantly, perhaps, we may then recover a practical sense of how our work as educational researchers constitutes and constrains the practice of education in schools, and thus make practical choices about how best to align ourselves with that work in order to improve it. To do this, I am sure, would be to follow in the tradition of educational research which Lawrence Stenhouse sought to establish.

Notes

This paper was The Lawrence Stenhouse Memorial Lecture delivered at the fifteenth annual conference of the British Educational Research Association, University of Newcastle Upon Tyne, 30 August–2 September 1989.
 1. Kuhn, T.S. (1970).
 2. Scriven, M. (1967: 30).
 3. Rudduck, J. (1988).
 4. Stenhouse, L.A. (1975).
 5. Stenhouse, L.A. (1983).
 6. For a collection of Stenhouse's writings on this theme, see Rudduck & Hopkins (1985).
 7. Though I cannot resist the temptation of pointing out that aspects of the 'teacher as researcher' idea are prefigured in *Culture and Education*. See especially Chapter 12, 'Conclusion: The training of teachers' and the (1971) 'Postscript: The Humanities Curriculum Project' in Stenhouse (1967). For example (from Chapter 12): 'Many of our current teaching problems, which are sometimes discussed as if they were entirely new, can be clarified by analysing carefully our past successes and understanding more clearly how they were achieved. Moreover, the innovations pioneered by teachers of exceptional talent can be generalised and assimilated only if they are subjected to close analytic scrutiny. Thus, the analysis of the teaching process and the development of a more vigorous critique of teaching are the fundamental tasks of educational theory' (p. 154). Or again (from the 1971 'Postscript'): 'Our experience in research and development in curriculum strongly underlines the need for much more emphasis on applied research in education . . . Much educational research places problems in a rational context without attacking them directly and effectively. When we move into the world of action, it does not stand us in good stead. . . . I am not arguing that a specification should control teachers, simply that it should communicate effectively. A teacher should be able to describe to a colleague what happens in his classroom. At the moment this does not seem possible. To make it possible we need more research which starts from practical situations. . . . Too many educationists are concerned with what ought to be done: too few are concerned with the problems of translating ideas into practice. Making educational ideas effective in the classroom seems to me more difficult—and at the same time even more worthwhile—than it did when I wrote this book four years ago' (p. 167).
 8. Stenhouse L.A. (1983) presents a collection of some of Stenhouse's major papers through the period.
 9. Stenhouse L.A. *et al.* (1982).
10. See, for example, 'Teaching through small-group discussion: Formality, rules and authority', originally published in 1972 in *The Cambridge Journal of Education* (vol. 2, no. 1, pp. 18–24) and reprinted in Stenhouse (1983).

11. Rudduck, J. (1988: 30).
12. For example, 'Curriculum research and the art of the teacher (originally delivered as an address to the 1978 Conference of the Association for the Study of the Curriculum, and first appearing in 1980 in *Curriculum*, vol. 1, no. 1, pp. 40–4) and his (February 1979) Inaugural Lecture at the University of East Anglia 'Research as a basis for teaching', both reprinted in Stenhouse (1983).
13. For example, Stenhouse, L.A. (1979a, 1980).
14. Stenhouse, L.A. (1979c).
15. Bartlett, L. and Kemmis, S. (1983).
16. See, for example, Stenhouse, L.A. (1978, 1979b).
17. Hoyle, E. (1972).
18. For example, in Carr, W. & Kemmis, S. (1986).
19. Stenhouse, L.A. (1975: 159, 163–5).
20. Stenhouse, L.A. (1983: 144).
21. See, for example, Elliott, J. & Adelman, C. (1973) and Elliott (1976–7).
22. Rudduck, J. & Hopkins, D. (1985).
23. Cf. Schwab, J.J. (1969). Schwab describes the second of six signs of crisis in the field of curriculum as: 'A flight upward, from discourse about the subject of the field to discourse about the the the discourse of the field, from *use* of principles and methods to *talk* about them, from grounded conclusions to the construction of models, from theory to metatheory and from metatheory to metametatheory.' The other signs of crisis are: (1) 'a flight of the field itself'; (3) 'a flight downwards, an attempt by practitioners to return to the subject matter in a state of innocence, shorn not only of curriculum principles but of all principles, in an effort to take a new, a pristine and unmediated look at the subject matter', (4) 'a flight to the sidelines, to the role of observer, commentator, historian, and critic of the contributions of others to the field'; (5) 'marked perseveration, a repetition of old and familiar knowledge in new languages which add little or nothing to the old meanings . . .'; and (6) 'a marked increase in eristic, contentious and *ad hominem* debate'.
24. From *An Introduction to Curriculum Research and Development* (Stenhouse, 1975: 5). Stenhouse offered this definition because he thought it 'does not make so many assumptions' (p. 5) as other standard definitions which he criticised. His own definition may or may not make fewer assumptions; it does make different assumptions.
25. It also suggests the Augustinian view of language criticised by Wittgenstein, which provided the point of departure for Wittgenstein's later theory of meaning as developing in interactions between people and the orientation of people (and language) to the world, formed in the mutually constitutive dynamism Wittgenstein described in terms of 'language games'. See Wittgenstein, L. (1974).
26. See Carr, W. (1980, 1986).
27. For example, McKeon, R. (1952) and Habermas, J. (1974).
28. See, for example, Winter, R. (1987). Winter makes a clear case for reflexivity as a central theoretical category in educational research, including educational action research.
29. This has been argued in Carr, W. & Kemmis, S. (1986) — see especially Chapter 4.
30. See MacIntyre, A. (1981), in particular, Chapter 14 'The nature of the virtues' and Chapter 15 'The virtues, the unity of a human life and the concept of tradition'.
31. See Hindess, B. (1977: 8): 'Rationalist epistemology conceives of the world as a rational order in the sense that its parts and the relations between them conform to concepts and the relations between them, the concept giving the essence of the real. Where rationalist epistemology presupposes an *a priori* correspondence, a pre-given harmony,

between ideas and the world, the rationalist conception of action postulates a mechanism of the realisation of ideas. For example, in Weber's conception of action as "oriented in its course" by meanings, the relation between action and meaning is one of coherence and logical consistency: the action realises the logical consequences of its meaning. Is it necessary to point out the theological affinities of this conception of action? While theology postulates God as the mechanism *par excellence* of the realisation of the work, the rationalist conception of action conceives of a lesser but not essentially dissimilar mechanism.'

32. Stenhouse, L.A. (1975: 2).
33. Stenhouse, L.A. (1975: 2).
34. Stenhouse, L.A. (1975: 3).
35. Just how deeply social theory has been ensnared in the rationalistic theories of action is only now becoming clear. For some recent commentaries, see also Fay, B. (1987: 86–98), and Habermas, J. (1987): for example, 318–31). From a very different standpoint, an account of the importance of, and recovery of practical reason in the theory of action can be found in MacIntyre (1981, 1988),
36. Stenhouse, L.A. (1971: 167).
37. See, for example, 'Curriculum research and the art of the teacher' in Stenhouse, L.A. (1983), especially pp. 159–61. Note, however, that it is here that Stenhouse refers to 'a dialectic of idea and practice not to be separated from change', coyly quoting Mao Zedong on learning about reality through the struggle to change it. His use of the idea of 'applied research' in education, captured in the title of the Centre at the University of East Anglia (as well as in his writings about educational research), also attests to a view about practice as the application of research, including, presumably, the research carried out by the applied researchers working at the Centre — this notion of 'applied research' fundamentally implies a rationalistic theory of action.
38. Stenhouse cites Schwab's 'the practical' in the bibliography of *An Introduction to Curriculum Research and Development*, but does not refer to it in the text. Though aware of Schwab's work on the notion of practical reasoning, it seems to have played no major part in his own reconstruction of the problems of educational research.
39. Though referring to Mao on the dialectic of theory and practice (Stenhouse, 1983: 159), he seems not to have grasped the implication that theory is intrinsic to practice (what makes it a practice rather than merely action or behaviour), and that practice is also intrinsic to theory (not only its object or subject-matter, but its *raison d'être*). Nor, for example, did Stenhouse fully grasp the importance of contradiction as a central theoretical category — a key feature of dialectical reasoning.
40. Though he argued against positivistic perspectives on generalisation, especially where arguing for case study methods and for history, and especially in contexts where he also wanted to assert the necessity of appealing to what Hexter (1972) called 'the second record' (the interpretative frame through which the historian makes sense of historical evidence), he appears to have accepted the false dichotomy of the general and particular, not seeing the general in the particular and the particular in the general. His reading of Marx as an M.Ed. student at Glasgow seems not to have led him to a Hegelian view of the dialectic, Marx's historical materialism, or Engel's dialectical materialism, nor, in any clear way, to accept the (social or political) implications of such views. Nor, through referring in passing (in Stenhouse, 1981) to Habermas's *Theory and Practice* (1974), does he anywhere suggest that the resources of critical theory and/or critical social science might provide means for breaking out of the problems of empiricism or instrumentalism in curriculum theory, especially in dealing with the problems of theorising action.

41. I can find no reason to suppose that Stenhouse had a view on the alleged distinction between micro- and macro-sociological phenomena or studies, let alone his view on the relationship between them. It is clear, however, that (at least at the time of writing *An Introduction to Curriculum Research and Development*) he believed that general theoretical statements would require building from the particularities of many cases. At that time, he wrote 'The first level of generalisation is thus the development of a general theoretical language. In this, professional researchers should be able to help. If teachers report their work in such a tradition, case studies will accumulate, just as they do in medicine. Professional research workers will have to master this material and scrutinise it for general trends. It is out of this task that general propositional theory will be developed' (p. 157). In the same spirit, he later proposed the accumulation of 'case records' as the basis for developing more general interpretations, including 'analytic surveys' which 'attempt to draw data together from case records to make retrospective generalisations across cases' (Stenhouse 1978: 37). Given his interest in the development of professional interpretation and judgement, both among teachers and academic educational researchers, however, there is reason to suppose that he would have felt some sympathy for Giddens's rejection of the distinction between the micro and macro in sociology, and that he might have revised some of his views on generalisation in the light of them. (On the micro and macro, see for example Giddens, 979: 76–7). Giddens's general theory of agency and structure might also have attracted Stenhouse, especially in suggesting ways in which questions about practice can be reconciled with questions about the structures which practice produces and is produced by. To make this accommodation, however, Stenhouse would have been obliged to overturn his empiricist leanings, and to have embraced a more dialectical mode of reasoning. The theory of agency and structure is developed into a more cohesive theoretical statement in Giddens (1984).

42. For example, (on practical reasoning) he would not only refer to writings on practical reasoning, however obliquely, but he would have acepted the centrality of teacher's reasoning about practical problems as a basis for their own educational theories (not just theorising); (on the dialectic of theory and practice) he would have accepted that it is as true to say that practice constitutes theory as it is to say that theory constitutes practice; (on generalisation) he would have rejected positivistic educational research on the grounds that it reifies practice as a precondition for generalising about it; and (on the distinction between the micro and the macro) he would have eschewed the notion that broad educational theories can have validity (even as sources of insight for teachers) without being theories which simultaneously comprehend and explain the particularities of action as manifestations of the agency of the actors and as manifestations of the general cultural, economic and political forms (ideology) of a society.

43. For example, in Stenhouse (1979c: 7).

44. Rudduck (1988: 37).

45. Stenhouse (1985: 29).

46. It also fosters the rationalistic view of theorising discussed earlier, emphasising the power of ideas to guide or even direct action, rather than the way action and the circumstances in which we find ourselves and our notions of what is possible.

47. Schon (1983).

48. Note that 'knowledge', in ordinary usage, has at least a double sense: what I 'know' (in the sense of 'what I think'), and 'what I know to be true' or 'justified true belief' (which requires a test — which is at least in principle public — that it can be justified as being true).

49. The means of knowledge become 'public' is not merely through 'publication' (in the ordinary sense of the word), as Alasdair MacIntyre (1981) has argued. On the

distinction between activities and practices, see p. 175; and on the distinction between activities and practices, see p. 175; and on the distinction between practices and institutions, see p. 181), it becomes 'public' by being accommodated to publicly shared criteria and traditions of practice: by reference to the lives, virtues and excellences of practitioners as the bearers of these traditions; and by reference to the work of institutions created in order to nurture and sustain these activities and the values, virtues and excellences they embody and express. We are only entitled to call a practice 'educational' by reference to such public criteria and shared traditions.

50. See MacIntyre (1988). On pp. 12–13, he writes: 'A tradition is an argument extended through time in which certain fundamental agreements are defined and redefined in terms of two kinds of conflict: those with critics and enemies external to the tradition who reject all or at least key parts of those fundamental agreements, and those internal, interpretative debates through which the meaning and rationale of the fundamental agreements come to be expressed and by whose progress a tradition is constituted. Such internal debates may on occasion destroy the basis of common fundamental agreement, so that either a tradition divides into two or more warring components, whose adherents are transformed into exernal critics of each other's positions, or else the tradition loses all coherence and fails to survive. It can also happen that two traditions, hitherto independent and even antagonistic, can come to recognise certain possibilities of fundamental agreement and reconstitute themselves as a single, more complex debate.

'To appeal to tradition is to insist that we cannot adequately identify either our own commitments or those of others in the argumentative conflicts of the present except by situating them within those histories which made them what they have now become.'

51. Of course these processes also have a private face. Individuals consider theoretical ideas and their implications for practice, drawing private conclusions about what to do in given circumstances, no doubt, but they do so with a conscious awareness that both theory and practice are open to judgement by others, in relation to publicly accessible criteria, and in the light of circumstances. At such times, individuals place themselves under the authority of traditions and under the judgement of history, and perhaps (more immediately and more concretely) under the auspices of institutions. Their work is no longer to be understood as private activity, but rather as the embodiment and realisation of educational ideals, values and traditions of which they and others (some close by, and some very distant from us) are bearers, and to which they are contemporary contributors. In short, individuals may reflect and act privately on their understandings of theory and practice, but the development of theory and practice depends on the conscious participation of individuals in a public process — in one form or another, in research as Stenhouse initially defined it. The development of theory and practice requires our participation as individuals, but at the same time makes us more than individuals — it makes us the bearers of traditions, responsible with others for continuing the debates through which the traditions may be defended and strengthened, or through which they may properly be laid to rest.

52. And one which MacIntyre is unlikely to accept, given his scathing passing comment on 'neo-Weberian organisation theorists and the heirs of the Frankfurt School' (of social science, among whom Habermas must undoubtedly be counted) who, says MacIntyre, 'unwittingly collaborate in the theatre of the present' by defining the self in terms of its relationship to bureaucracy, despite their criticisms of bureaucratic modes of organisation and consciousness. See MacIntyre (1981: 29).

53. See, for example, Habermas (1970: 372).

54. See McCarthy (1975). McCarthy outlines the kinds of practices of communication characteristic of Habermas's ideal speech situation, drawing attention to the key

contention that the conditions for truth telling are also the conditions for democratic disucssion: 'The very act of participating in the discourse, of attempting discursively to come to an agreement about the truth of a problematic statement or the correctness of a problematic norm, carries with it the presupposition that a genuine agreement is possible. If we did not suppose that a justified consensus were possible and could in some way be distinguished from a false consensus, then the very meaning of discourse, indeed of speech, would be called into question. In attempting to come to a 'rational' decision about such matters, we must suppose that the outcome of our discussion will be the result simply of the force of the better argument, and not of accidental or systematic constraints on discussion. Habermas's thesis is that the structure [of communication] is free from constraint only when for all participants there is a symmetrical distribution of chances to select and employ speech acts, when there is an effective equality of chances to assume dialogue roles. In particular, all participants must have the same chance to initiate or perpetuate discourse, to put forward, to call into question, and give reasons for and against statements, interpretations, explanations and justifications. Furthermore, they must have the same chance to express attitudes, feelings, intentions and the like, and to command, to oppose, to permit, and to forbid, etc. In other words, the conditions of the ideal speech situation must ensure discussion which is free from all constraints of domination. Thus, the conditions for ideal discourse are connected with conditions for an ideal form of life; they include linguistic conceptualisations of the traditional ideas of freedom and justice. "Truth", therefore, cannot be analysed independently of "freedom" and "justice"' (p.xvii).

55. For a detailed exposition of the theory of agency and structure, see Giddens (1984). On ideology, see Giddens (1979), especially Chapter 5, 'Ideology and Consciousness'.

56. For which he argued most forcefully in his February 1977 Inaugural Lecture at the University of East Anglia, 'Research as a basis for teaching', in Stenhouse (1983).

57. For example: 'The crucial problem for curriculum research and study is the development of theory and methodology which is subservient to the needs of teachers and schools. This means that the theory has to be accessible. And it means that the personnel who identify themselves with this field should not allow themselves — or be allowed — to use their knowledge and expertise to divide themselves from teachers. When it comes to proving oneself as a researcher, the school is often a less attractive setting than the international conference. There is a place for the latter, but not as a substitute for the former.' (Stenhouse, 1975: 207).

58. For example: 'I believe that fruitful development in the field of curriculum and teaching depends upon evolving styles of co-operative research by teachers and using full-time researchers to support the teachers' work. This probably means that research reports and hypotheses must be addressed to teachers, that is, they must invite classroom research responses rather than laboratory research responses.' (Stenhouse, 1975: 162).

59. A marked exception is Jack Whitehead, who has repeatedly stressed that educational theorists have a first duty to explain, interpret and act upon their own analyses of the contradictions in their own educational practices. He invites educational researchers to explore 'I as a living contradiction'. See, for example, Whitehead (1984).

60. An example of an exception to this generalisation is Hamilton (1977). A well-known example from sociology is Geer (1964).

61. Carr & Kemmis (1986). See especially, Chapter 4, 'Theory and practice: Redefining the problem'.

62. See Foucault (1980).

63. See Foucault (1970).

64. See Foucault (1979).
65. Foucault (1979: 190).
66. Foucault (1985: 13).
67. This was part of the theme of John Elliott's First Lawrence Stenhouse Memorial Lecture (Elliott, 1988). (See Chapter 4, this volume.)
68. Stenhouse (1975: 166).
69. Stenhouse (1975: 185).
70. Stenhouse (1975: 215).
71. Stenhouse (1975: 215).
72. Cremin (1961).
73. Stenhouse (1975: 196).
74. Stenhouse (1975: 207–8).
75. Stenhouse (1975: 196).
76. Stenhouse argued that the failures in Schon's 'proliferation of centres' model of curriculum innovation could be attributed to the defects of movements: 'Within limits it [Schon's model] is a good model in the areas of political and social policy. However, my argument throughout this book has been that a central problem in the improvement of education is the gap between accepted policy and practice. Policy is too often out of touch with reality. The problem is that the movement's learning capacity is largely instrumental. The direction of the movement is assumed and its learning is learning of tactics. Within its structure there is no systematic basis for the critical development of either the message or its practical implementation in classrooms. The desideratum in educational innovation is less that we improve our tactics in advancing our cause than that we improve our capacity to criticise our practice in the light of our beliefs and our beliefs in the light of our practice. It is this that points to the need for a research tradition which can temper the confidence of movements'. (Stenhouse, 1975: 218–19).
77. It is ironic, in the light of Stenhouse's resistance to the idea of movements, that educational action-research in Britain, which flowered from Stenhouse's notion of the teacher as researcher, should be described as a movement, for example in Elliott (1989). Nevertheless, Elliott is right about this: it is a movement, and it is in productive tension with the social ordering of education. I am less certain about the 'creative compromise' Elliott describes ·in the 'two-tier' model of teacher appraisal, in which the first tier is based on action research by teachers. It seems to me that the location of this 'tier' under a state-controlled upper 'tier', puts it at considerable risk of co-option. Whether this is so or not, the action research 'tier' offers the possibility of resistance (as Elliott points out) — especially if it is collaboratively organised, and offers possibilities for linking teachers within and across schools and education authorities.
78. See Touraine (1981).
79. In particular through the work of Schwab and others (such as Walker and Reid) in the tradition of 'the practical', and later, through the work of people following the lines of critical theory in educational research. See, for example, Schwab (1970), Reid (1978), Walker (1971), Bredo & Feinberg (1982), Feinberg (1983), Carr & Kemmis (1986).
80. He refers to Schwab's 'The practical', for example, but makes no clear use of it; he refers to Habermas's (1974) *Theory and Practice* as 'one of the most famous recent attempts to relate theory and practice' (Stenhouse 1981: 44) but makes no further conspicuous use of metatheory or critical theory.
81. See Giddens (1979), especially Chapter 5, 'Ideology and consciousness'.
82. See Carr & Kemmis (1986: 215–16) 'The separation of theory and practice endemic to positivist and interpretivist views of research is now institutionalised in a division

of labour between "theorists" and "practitioners". The task of eliminating any inadequacies in practitioners' conceptions of educational practice is not, therefore, merely a task of revealing any personal misconceptions that may accidentally have been picked up. It is also a task of freeing them from misconceptions systematically developed, promulgated and sustained in the dominant forms of educational research and educational policy. The epistemological separation of educational theory from educational practice has its social counterpart in the separation of educational researchers and policy-makers on the one hand from educational practitioners on the other.'

83. In this context, it is well worth returning to the distinctions between 'bureaucratic', 'automatic' and 'democratic' evaluation introduced by MacDonald (1976). The descriptions of the working relationships between these different kinds of evaluators and sponsors, officials, academic communities and programme participants are of particular interest from the perspective of a concept of metapractice in educational evaluation.

84. See MacIntyre (1983: 181) 'Practices must not be confused with institutions. Chess, physics and medicine are practices; chess clubs, laboratories, universities and hospitals are institutions. Institutions are characteristically and necessarily concerned with what I have called external goods. They are involved in acquiring money and other material goods; they are structured in terms of power and status, and they distribute money, power and status as rewards. Nor could they do otherwise if they are to sustain not only themselves, but also the practices of which they are the bearers. For no practices can survive for any length of time unsustained by institutions. Indeed so intimate is the relationship of practices to institutions — and consequently of the goods external to the goods internal to the practices in question — that institutions and practices characteristically form a single causal order in which the ideals and the creativity of the practice are always vulnerable to the acquisitiveness of the institution, in which the co-operative care for the common goods of the practice is always vulnerable to the competitiveness of the institution. In this context, the essential purpose of the virtues is clear. Without them, without justice, courage and truthfulness, practices could not resist the corrupting power of institutions.'

85. Perhaps the most celebrated example is MacDonald (1976), but there are now many other works in this tradition. Other people who are, or have been, members of the Centre for Applied Research in Education who have written on the topic include John Elliott, David Jenkins, Stephen Kemmis, Saville Kushner, Nigel Norris, Helen Simons, Lawrence Stenhouse, and Rob Walker. Arguably, some of these people developed their interest in the topic after thinking through the implications of Stenhouse's idea of 'neutral chairmanship' in the context of the Humanities Curriculum Project. Others formed their interest in it after working with MacDonald on the notion of 'democratic evaluation'.

86. Parsons (1976).

87. Reynolds (1980–81).

88. See especially Habermas (1972).

89. See Carr & Kemmis (1986).

90. See, for example, Thompson & McCarthy (1982).

91. See especially the section 'Against "Micro" and "Macro": Social and system integration' (pp. 139–44) in Chapter 3.

92. A shortcoming which has characterised some of my own writings on action research and the formation of critical communities of practitioners. The 'political' solution of more open and equal relationships must be supplemented and qualified by a substantive

solution: it is not just that the work is done democratically that it is important, it is also what the work is, and what its consequences are.
93. David Hamilton (1989) provides powerful insights into the relationship between pedagogical forms and social, cultural, economic and political structures over some centuries. The kind of analysis described there can and should be made of educational research, especially over the last century.
94. Althusser (1971).
95. Fals Borda (1979).

References

Althusser, Louis (1971) *Lenin and Philosophy and Other Essays* (trans B. Brewster). London: New Left Books.
Bartlett, Leo and Kemmis, Stephen (eds) (1983) *Perspectives on Case Study, vol. 2: The Quasi-Historical Approach.* Geelong, Victoria: Deakin University Press.
Bredo, Eric and Feinberg, Walter (eds.) (1982) *Knowledge and Values in Social and Educational Research.* Philadelphia, Pa: Temple University Press.
Carr, Wilfred (1980) The 'gap' between theory and practice. *Journal of Further and Higher Education* 4, 60–9.
  – (1986) Theories of theory and practice. *Journal of Philosophy of Education* 20 (2), 177–86.
Carr, Wilfred and Kemmis, Stephen (1986) *Becoming Critical: Education, Knowledge and Action Research.* London: Falmer.
Cremin, Lawrence A. (1961) *The Transformation of the School.* New York: Alfred A. Knopf.
Elliott, John (1976–7) Developing hypotheses about classrooms from teachers' practical constructs: An account of the Ford Teaching Project. *Interchange.* 7 (2), 2–20.
  – (1988) Education in the shadow of the Education Reform Act. The Lawrence Stenhouse Memorial Lecture delivered at the Annual Conference of the British Educational Research Association, University of East Anglia, September. (See Chapter 4, this volume.)
  – (1989) The emergence of teacher appraisal in the UK. Paper presented at the Annual Meeting of the American Educational Research Association, San Francisco, March.
Elliott, John and Adelman, Clem (1973) Reflecting where the action is: The design of the Ford Teaching Project. *Education for Teaching,* 92, 8–20.
Fals Borda, Orlando (1979) Investigating reality in order to transform it: The Colombian experience. *Dialectical Anthropology* 4, March, 33–55. (Reprinted in McTaggart, Robin and Kemmis, Stephen (eds) (1988) *The Action Research Reader,* 3rd edn. Geelong, Victoria: Deakin University Press.)
Fay, Brian (1987) *Critical Social Science.* Cambridge: Polity Press.
Feinberg, Walter (1983) *Understanding Education: Towards a Reconstruction of Educational Inquiry.* Cambridge: Cambridge University Press.
Foucault, Michel (1970) *The Order of Things: An Archaeology of the Human Sciences.* London: Tavistock.
  – (1979) *Discipline and Punish.* Harmondsworth, Middlesex: Penguin.
  – (1980) *Power/Knowledge: Selected Interviews and Other Writings* (ed. Colin Gordon; trans C. Gordon et al.). Hassocks, Sussex: Harvester Press.
  – (1985) Questions of method: An interview with Michel Foucault. *Ideology and Consciousness* 8, Spring, 3–14. *
Geer, Blanche (1964) First days in the field. In P.E. Hammond (ed.) *Sociologists at Work: Essays on the Craft of Social Research* (pp. 322–44). New York: Basic Books.

Giddens, Anthony (1979) *Central Problems in Social Theory: Action, Structure and Contradiction in Social Analysis*. London: MacMillan Education.
— (1984) *The Constitution of Society*. Cambridge: Polity Press.
Habermas, Jürgen (1970) Towards a theory of communicative competence. *Inquiry* 13.
— (1972) *Knowledge and Human Interests* (trans Jeremy J. Shapiro). London: Heinemann.
— (1974) *Theory and Practice* (trans John Viertel). London: Heinemann.
— (1987) *The Theory of Communicative Action, Vol II; Lifeworld and System: A Critique of Functionalist Reason* (trans Thomas McCarthy). Boston, MA: Beacon Press.
Hamilton, David (1977) A methodological diary. In Nigel Norris (ed.) *Theory in Practice* (pp. 136–46). University of East Anglia Centre for Applied Research in Education.
— (1989) *Towards a Theory of Schooling*. London: Falmer Press.
Hexter, J.H. (1972) *The History Primer*. London: Penguin.
Hindess, Barry (1977) *Philosophy and Methodology in the Social Sciences*. Hassocks, Sussex: Harvester Press.
Hoyle, Eric (1972) Creativity in the school. Unpublished paper presented at the OECD Workshop on Creativity of the School, Estoril, Portugal.
Kuhn, Thomas S. (1970) *The Structure of Scientific Revolutions*, 2nd edn. Chicago: University of Chicago Press.
McCarthy, Thomas (1975) Translator's Introduction. In Jürgen Habermas *Legitimation Crisis*. Boston, MA: Beacon Press.
MacDonald, Barry (1976) Evaluation and the control of education. In David Tawney (ed.) *Curriculum Evaluation Today: Trends and Implications*. London: Macmillan Education.
MacIntyre, Alasdair (1981) *After Virtue: A Study in Moral Theory*. London: Duckworth.
McKeon, Richard (1952) Philosophy and action. *Ethics* LXII (2), 79–100.
Parsons, Carl (1976) The new evaluation: A cautionary note. *Journal of Curriculum Studies* 8 (2), 125–38.
Reid, William (1978) *Thinking about the Curriculum: The Nature and Treatment of Curriculum Problems*. London: Routledge & Kegan Paul.
Reynolds, D. (1980–81) The naturalistic method of educational and social research: A Marxist critique. *Interchange* 11 (4), 77–89.
Rudduck, Jean (1988) Changing the world of the classroom by understanding it: A review of some aspects of the work of Lawrence Stenhouse. *Journal of Curriculum and Supervision*, 4 (1), 30–42.
Rudduck, Jean and Hopkins, David (eds) (1985) *Research as a Basis for Teaching: Readings from the Work of Lawrence Stenhouse*. Heinemann: London.
Schon, Donald A. (1983) *The Reflective Practitioner: How Professionals Think in Action*. London: Temple Smith.
Schwab, Joseph J. (1969) The practical: A language for curriculum. *School Review* 78 (1), 1–23.
— (1970) *The Practical: A Language for Curriculum*. Washington DC: Schools for the 70s auxiliary series, National Education Association Centre for the Study of Instruction.
Scriven, Michael (1967) The methodology of evaluation. In R.E. Stake (ed.) *Perspectives of Curriculum Evaluation* (pp. 39–83), No. 1, AERA Monograph Series on Curriculum Evaluation. Washington DC: American Educational Research Association.
Stenhouse, Lawrence A. (1971) *Culture and Education*. (First published 1967.) London: Nelson University Paperback Edition.
— (1975) *An Introduction to Curriculum Research and Development*. London: Heinemann.
— (1978) Case study and case records: towards a contemporary history of education. *British Journal of Educational Research* 4 (2), 21–39.

— (1979a) Case study and comparative education: Particularity and generalization. *Comparative Education* 15 (2), 5–10.
— (1979b) Library access, library use and user education in academic sixth forms. Proposal to the British Library Research and Development Department. University of East Anglia, Norwich: Centre for Applied Research in Education.
— (1989c) The problems of standards in illuminative research. *Scottish Educational Review* 11 (1), 5–10.
— (1980) The study of samples and the study of cases. *British Educational Research Journal* 6 (1), 1–6.
— (1981) Case study in educational research and evaluation, paper delivered at the symposium Fallstudien in der Pädagogik, Comenius Institut, West Germany, September. Reprinted in Leo Bartlett and Stephen Kemmis (eds) (1983) *Case Study: An Overview,* 2nd edn. Geelong, Victoria: Deakin University Press.
— (1983) *Authority, Education and Emancipation.* London: Heinemann.
— (1985) Applying research to education. In Jean Rudduck and David Hopkins (eds) *Research as a Basis for Teaching: Readings from the Work of Lawrence Stenhouse.* London: Heinemann.
Stenhouse, Lawrence A., Verma, Gajendra, Wild, Robert, and Nixon, Jon (1982) *Teaching about Race Relations: Problems and Effects.* London: Routledge & Kegan Paul.
Thompson, J.B. and McCarthy, Thomas (eds) (1982) *Habermas: Critical Debates.* London: Macmillan.
Touraine, Alain (1981) *The Voice and the Eye: An Analysis of Social Movements.* Cambridge: Cambridge University Press.
Walker, Decker F. (1971) A naturalistic model for curriculum development. *School Review* 80, 51–65.
Whitehead, Jack (1984) The creation and testing of a living form of educational theory from educational action-research enquiries. Unpublished paper, School of Education, University of Bath.
Winter, Richard (1987) *Action-Research and the Nature of Social Inquiry: Professional Innovation and Educational Work.* Aldershot: Avebury Press.
Wittgenstein, Ludwig (1974) *Philosophical Investigations* (trans. G.E.M. Anscombe). Oxford: Basil Blackwell.